GW00632703

WORD 6
FOR WINDOWS
in easy steps

1997

SCOTT BASHAM

COMPUTER STEP

First published November 1994

Computer Step
5c Southfield Road
Southam
Warwickshire CV33 OJH
England

Tel. 01926 817999
Fax. 01926 817005

Notice of Liability

Every effort has been made to ensure that this book contains accurate and current information. However, Computer Step and the author shall not be liable for any loss or damage suffered by readers as a result of any information contained herein.

Trademarks

Microsoft and MS are registered trademarks and Windows and Windows NT are trademarks of Microsoft Corporation. All other trademarks are acknowledged as belonging to their respective companies.

British Library Cataloguing in Publication Data

A catalogue record for this book is available from the British Library.

Printed in England

ISBN 1 874029 16 4

About the Author

Scott Basham has a BSc. in Computer Science from the University of Edinburgh. Since then he has lived and worked in Edinburgh, spending several years as a computing lecturer.

In 1990 he moved to Aldus U.K. (now Adobe Systems), working firstly as a Training Consultant before moving into course development.

Today he works as a freelance Training Consultant and Author. He has produced training materials for a wide variety of PC and Macintosh application packages, as well as courses covering computer theory ranging from basic to advanced levels. He regularly runs training courses in Word, PageMaker, FreeHand, PhotoStyler and Persuasion for clients which include BP, Mistsubishi, Canon, Apple, The Bank of Scotland, Wang, SoftSell, P&P and the BBC.

He has also written "PageMaker 5 in Easy Steps" in this same series of books - see last page.

In what he laughingly calls his spare time, he writes, records and performs original music. This too involves him spending ridiculous number of hours wrestling with computer technology.

Table of Contents

7. Structured Text   61

8. Automatic Features   71

9. Styles   91

10. Templates   105

11. The Organizer   115

CHAPTER

1

The Word
Screen

THIS CHAPTER COVERS

in easy Steps

Introduction

Word Processing was one of the first popular applications for the modern personal computer. In the early days, even though it provided little more than the ability to enter and change text on a computer monitor, it was eagerly adopted by those of us who were frustrated by the inflexibility and unforgiving nature of typewriters.

As time went on software and hardware improved, and features such as spell checking and various type effects were added. Also, the number of users increased.

Today the most popular personal computer configuration is the IBM PC compatible with the Microsoft Windows graphical operating environment. Microsoft, the world's largest software manufacturer, provides a complete range of applications, including spreadsheet, database, graphics and presentation software. Microsoft Word for Windows, in its latest incarnation (Version 6), is widely acknowledged as a leader in its field, and is one of the best selling packages in any software category.

Let's face it, with Word we're talking about a *big* package. It has retained the position as market leader by stuffing itself full of useful features, taking it from Word Processing into the realms of graphical and data-oriented documents. At first it may seem to contain a bewildering array of options and controls, but many are there to make life easier – providing quick access to the most commonly used features.

A big package inevitably comes with a depressingly big reference manual, which will describe each and every function in minute detail. This book is not intended to replace the manual, instead you should view it as a more graphical teaching guide. Wherever possible I've used pictures and examples rather than pages of text to explain and demonstrate the concepts covered.

To gain maximum benefit from this book, I recommend two things:

- Make sure that you are first familiar with the Windows operating environment (i.e. using a mouse, icons, menus, dialog boxes etc.). Look at the appropriate *Windows in Easy Steps* title in this same series of books for help with Windows itself.

- Remember that it is also important to experiment using your own examples; like many things you will find that practice is the key to competence.

Starting Word

TIP

*Typing "**WIN
WINWORD**" at
the DOS prompt
will launch
Windows and then
Word.*

From the Program Manager, you can start Word by double
clicking directly on its icon.

Alternatively, from the File Manager locate the
WINWORD.EXE file and double click.

NOTE

*If you double click on a file with a **.DOC** extension, then your machine will
load Word and then automatically open the file.*

Tip of the Day

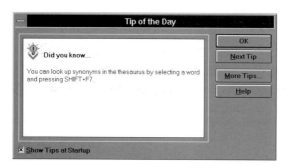

Usually Word will display the "Tip of the Day" message box at
this point. If you don't wish to see this, switch off the checkbox
at its lower left corner.

The Word Screen

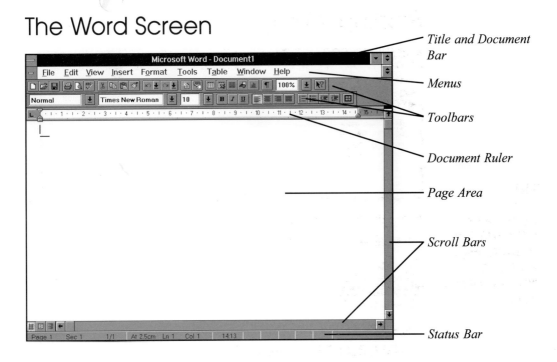

Title and Document Bar

Menus

Toolbars

Document Ruler

Page Area

Scroll Bars

Status Bar

If you have just opened Word, you'll see something like this. Don't worry if there are extra items or things missing from this diagram, you'll see in a moment that it's possible to configure the Word screen in different ways.

Toolbars

Toolbars can appear at the top of the screen, at the bottom, or as floating palettes. They give you instant access to features without the need to search through menus and dialog boxes. There are eight Toolbars in total, but we usually only require a couple at any time.

Activating/Deactivating Toolbars

1. Go to the View menu and choose Toolbars...

TIP

A quick way to switch Toolbars on and off is to hold down the right Mouse button whilst within any currently visible Toolbar.

2. Make sure that all are switched off except for "Standard" and "Formatting".

These are all you'll need for now.

Adjusting the Page Setup

1. Go to the File menu and choose "Page Setup".

The Page Setup dialog box appears.

click here if necessary to see the Margins settings

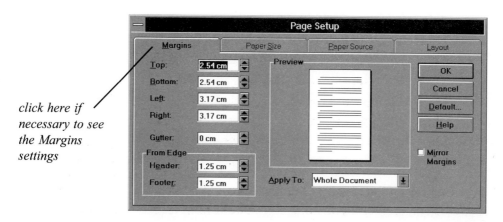

◁

Tabbed Dialog Boxes

Many of Word's dialog boxes are *tabbed*, i.e. subdivided into sections. You can select your required section by clicking on the tab at the top of the box.

2.	Now click on the "Paper Size" tab:

click here

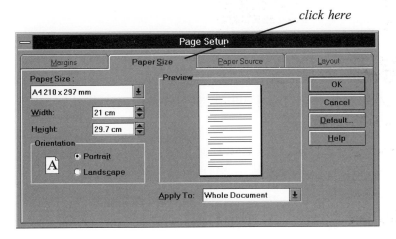

Tabbed dialog boxes are used in Word wherever there is a large number of settings to change.

TIP

You can also select tabs pressing the Alt key together with the underlined letter in the Tab name.

Alternatively, pressing Control together with the TAB key itself will cycle through each Tab in turn.

help box ─── Normal View

Changes the editing view to normal view

Help

If you allow your Mouse pointer to rest over an icon for a moment, a help box will appear. This gives you a brief explanation of the icon's function. In addition to this, the Status bar at the bottom of the screen will give a longer description.

You can also access the on-line Help (from the Help menu), or use the Help icon ▶? at the top right of the screen. Click on this, then click on an icon or menu option to make the relevant help text appear.

NOTE

If you press the F1 key while in a dialog box, then you'll see Help text about its options.

Page Views

There are four different ways of viewing the page, selectable from the top section of the View menu.

Alternatively, you can use the icons immediately to the left of the horizontal scroll bars.

The view icons:
Normal, Page Layout and ——
Outline respectively

The Page Views

HINT

*Use Normal page
view unless you
have a specific
reason to choose
one of the others.*

- Normal: Allows fast editing, previewing most (but not all) text effects.

- Outline: Views your text as a structured Outline (see chapter 15 "The Outline View" for more details).

- Page Layout: Displays your document as actual pages, previewing text and graphics effects.

- Master Document: A special form of Outline view, used for long or structured documents (see chapter 23 "Advanced Features" for more information).

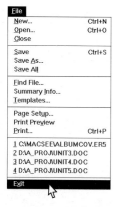

Leaving Word

You can exit from Word in the normal way by

- Choosing "Exit" from the File menu.

or

- Double-clicking on the Control menu box in the extreme top-left corner of the Word Window.

CHAPTER

2

Basic Text Manipulation

THIS CHAPTER COVERS

in easy steps

The Document Window

1. If there is no document window, then create a new one by clicking on the "New" icon in the top left of the standard Toolbar.

The New document icon

2. Enter a sentence of example text.

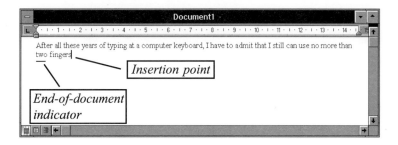

The vertical line is your Insertion Point, indicating where new text will appear. You can move the Insertion Point by:

*   Using the Cursor (arrow) keys.

*   Clicking a new position with the Mouse.

*   For other methods refer to Chapter 5 "Working with a Document".

NOTE

Word automatically works out when to take a new line without breaking words. However, if you want to start a new paragraph, press the Return or Enter key.

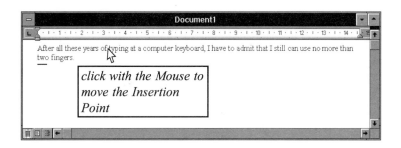

3. Move the Insertion Point to a point where you would wish to add more text.

Inserting Text

4.   Type the text. It will appear at the Insertion Point.

Note that the words to the right of the Insertion Point move along to accommodate the new text:

Deleting Text using Backspace

5.   Move the Insertion Point so that it is directly after the text you want to delete.

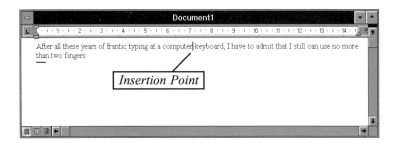

6.   Press the Backspace key once to erase each character to the left of the Insertion Point.

Deleting Text with the Delete Key

7.   This time move the Insertion Point before the text to be
      deleted.

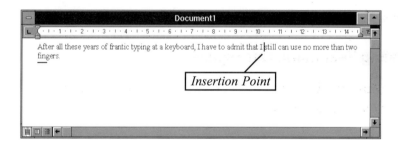

8.   Press the Delete key once for each character to be deleted.

Selecting Text

9. You can select text by dragging horizontally across it using the Mouse:

Replacing Selected Text

10. Anything you type will automatically replace any text which is currently selected:

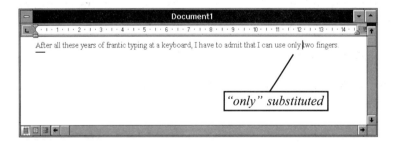

Adding More Text to the End of the Document

11. Remember that before adding more text to the end of your document, you must first reposition the Insertion Point:

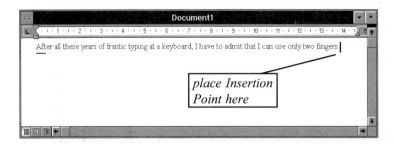

Note that, to start a new line at the end of the document, you must first click at the end of the last line.

12.   Add the text:

Insert versus Overtype

At the bottom of the screen, in the Status bar, the letters "OVR" should be greyed out. This indicates that we are in Insert, rather than Overtype mode.

13.   Press the Insert key several times.

Each time you do this, the "OVR" indicator will select or deselect.

14.   If necessary, press Insert again to activate Overtype mode.

In Overtype mode, new text overtypes (replaces) any text to the right of the Insertion Point.

15.   Position the Insertion Point somewhere within your text:

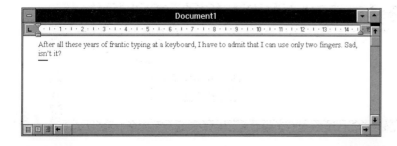

16.   Type some new text.

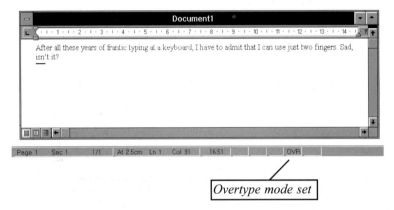

Overtype mode set

17.   Use the Insert key to switch back to Insert mode.

Better Ways to Select Text

18.   Choose the "Select All" option from the Edit Menu (or
        type Control + A).

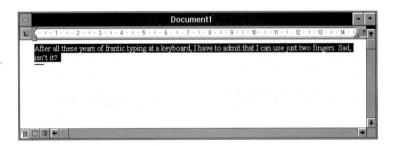

Changing the Appearance of Text

19.   Open the "size" pop-up menu from the Toolbar, and increase the point size of the text to double its previous value.

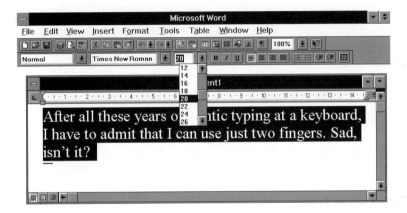

20.   Select a single word and use the toolbar to switch on the Bold effect.

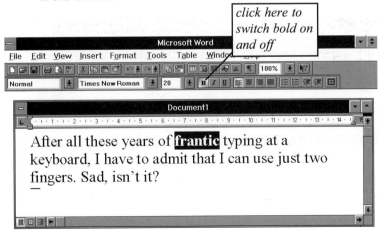

TIP

The keyboard shortcut for Bold is Control + Shift + B

21. If you want to select text over more than one line, either
     drag over the area required or click at one end of the
     selection, then hold down Shift and click at the other end:

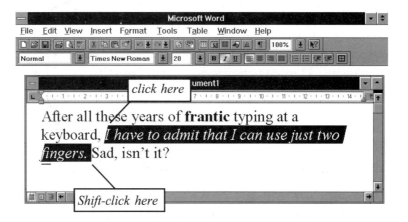

click here

Shift-click here

22. You can also select whole lines of text by dragging
     vertically over the area within the left margin.

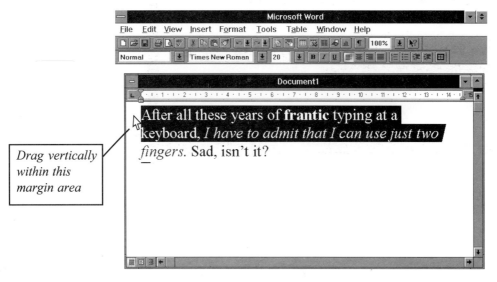

*Drag vertically
within this
margin area*

23.   You can also double-click to select a single word...

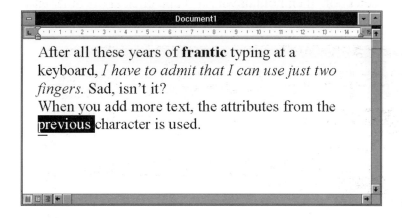

24.   ...or triple-click to select an entire paragraph:

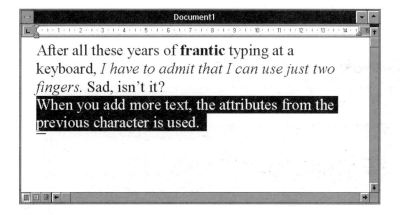

25. Note that if you click an Insertion Point and then type more text, the new text takes its attributes (appearance) from the previous character.

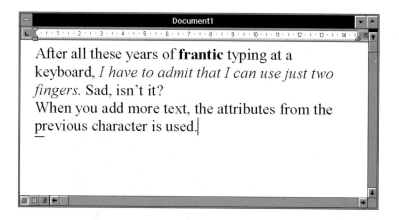

Saving a Document

1. To Save your work either choose "Save" from the File menu, or click on the Save icon in the Toolbar.

The Save icon

The following dialog box will appear:

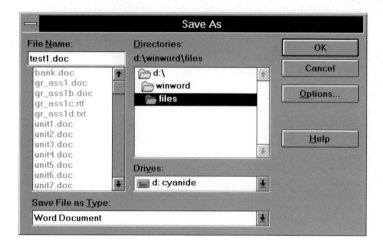

2. If necessary, select the correct drive and directory.

3. Enter the filename and click "OK".

4. If you have finished with the document, choose "Close" from the File menu.

Opening a Document

Either

- Choose "Open" from the File menu or click on the Open icon:

the Open icon

Or

- The last few files used are listed in the lower section of the File menu, and can be selected directly.

Printing a Document

1.   Either choose "Print" from the File menu, or click on the
      Print icon in the Toolbar:

   the Print icon

The following dialog box will appear:

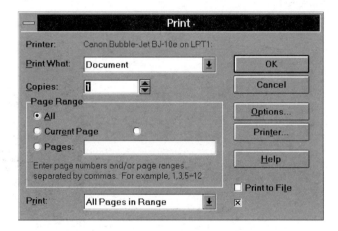

2.   Enter the number of copies required.

3.   Click "OK" to go ahead, or "Cancel" to abort.

Character Level
Formatting

THIS CHAPTER COVERS

In easy steps

Character Level Formatting

What does "Character level" mean?

Character level attributes include font name, size, emboldening, underlining plus all sorts of other effects which can be applied to individual characters. If required, every single character could be given different attributes (although this would tend to make our document look a little like a ransom letter).

Using the Formatting Toolbar

1.   Select the text which you want to format.

2.   Choose the font required from the pop-up menu in the toolbar:

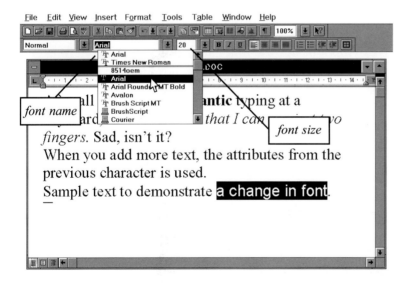

A font is a collection of characters with a particular visual style. Common fonts include:

Times or Times New Roman (useful for main text)

Helvetica (useful for headings)

Courier (the typewriter font)

3.   Look at the font names in the pop-up list:

*The most recently used fonts appear
above this line*

TrueType symbol

Printer icon

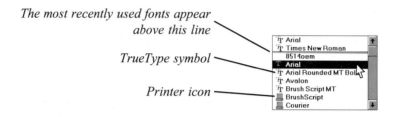

•   A printer icon beside the name indicates a printer-font.
        Your machine will use the closest available screen font
        (which may not match the printed output exactly).

•   A double T symbol indicates a TrueType font, which is
        used for both screen display and printing.

•   No symbol beside the font name indicates a screen font.
        Always check that your printer can reproduce this to a high
        enough quality.

4.   You can use the buttons on this Toolbar to add effects
        such as bold, italic and underline:

TIP

*If you highlight a
portion of text, the
toolbar will
indicate its current
formatting options.*

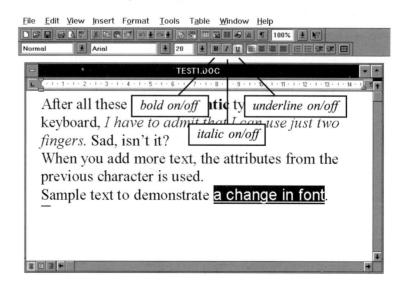

The Font Dialog Box

This controls all aspects of character level formatting.

1. Select the text to change.

2. Either choose "Font" from the Format menu, or click your right Mouse button inside the document window:

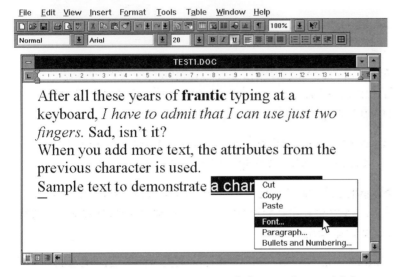

This brings up a pop-up menu containing options which are relevant to the task in hand. Later you will see that it changes depending on your current context.

3. Choose "Font".

The following dialog box appears:

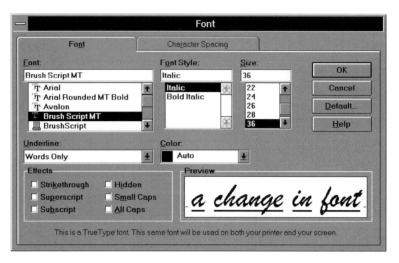

4. Experiment with the different options, noting how they affect the Preview image.

5. Click on the Character Spacing tab.

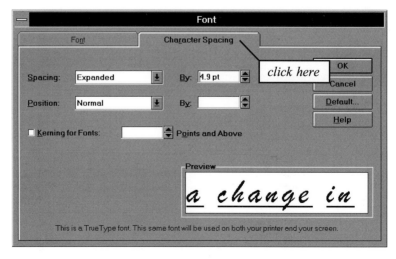

From here you can numerically control the character spacing, the position (for superscript and subscript), and kerning.

Kerning

Certain pairs of letters look odd with normal character spacing. Word uses kerning tables, which tell it how much closer together to bring them.

e.g.

To *unkerned*

To *kerned*

This process of examining each pair of adjacent character in the document would slow down your machine considerably, so if you activate kerning you should set a threshold of approximately 12 points.

This means that Word will only consider text larger than 12 points for kerning. Spacing in small text is not so noticeable, so this will speed things up without a marked deterioration in quality.

To activate kerning:

1.   Switch on the "Kerning for Fonts" checkbox.

2.   Set the "Points and Above" value.

Changing Font Quickly

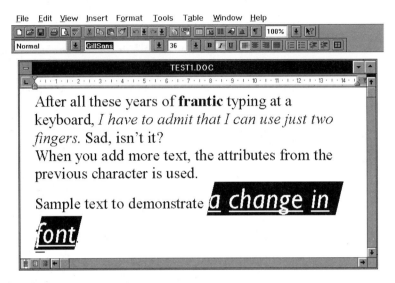

1.   Select the text.

2.   Press Control + Shift + F.

3.   Type the first few letters of the font and press the Down
      Arrow key. You need to type enough letters to distinguish
      the font name from any others which may be similar.

4.   Press Return.

HINT

*Pressing Control + Shift + F twice is another quick way of accessing the
Font dialog box.*

CHAPTER

4

Paragraph Level Formatting

THIS CHAPTER COVERS

in easy steps

Paragraph Level Formatting

What does "Paragraph level" mean?

Options such as alignment, left and right indents, and space above and below refer to whole paragraphs, i.e. each paragraph has only one set of these attributes.

Formatting with the Toolbar

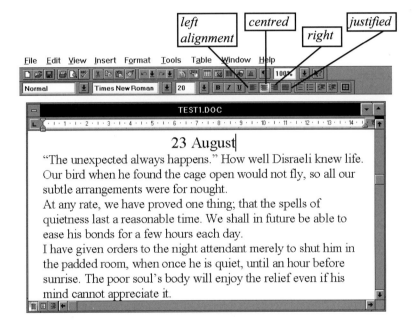

1. Select the paragraph(s) to format. Remember that a heading is often a single line paragraph.

2. Choose the form of alignment by clicking on the appropriate tool in the formatting toolbar.

NOTE

If you are changing just one paragraph you need only click an Insertion Point somewhere within it. Any change to a paragraph-level attribute will always affect the entire paragraph surrounding the Insertion Point.

Forms of Alignment

There are four forms of alignment:

Left

Text lines up along its left edge, with a ragged right edge.

Right

Here the text is moved so that the right edge is straight, and the left is ragged.

Centre

Text is centred between the left and right edges.

Justification

The text spacing is adjusted so that each line within a paragraph begins and ends in the same position (dictated by the margins and indents), giving a neat and regular appearance. Below is an example of justified text:

NOTE

The last line of each paragraph is only aligned left, allowing the reader to easily distinguish one paragraph from another.

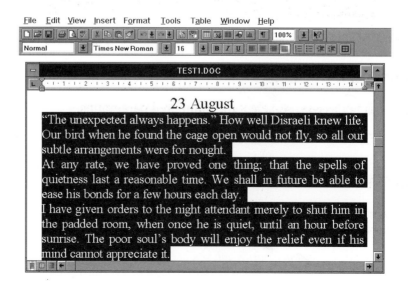

Numbered Paragraphs

Activating Numbers

1. Select the paragraphs to be numbered.

2. Click on the Numbering icon in the formatting toolbar:

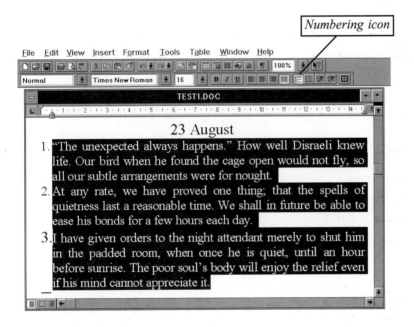

Removing Numbers

1. If necessary, re-select the numbered paragraphs.

2. Click on the Numbering icon a second time.

NOTE

The numbering options will be examined in greater detail in Chapter 7 "Structured Text".

Bulleted Paragraphs

Activating Numbers

1. Select the paragraphs to be bulleted.

2. Click on the Bullet icon in the formatting toolbar:

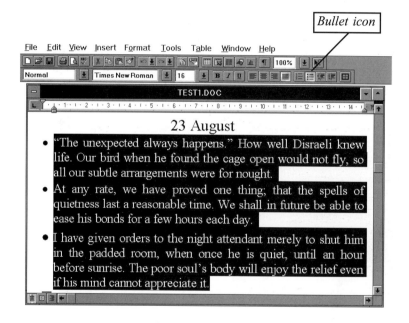

Bullet icon

Removing Bullets

1. If necessary, re-select the numbered paragraphs.

2. Click on the Bullet icon a second time.

NOTE

The bulleted text options will be examined in greater detail in Chapter 7 "Structured Text".

The Paragraph Dialog Box

This controls all aspects of paragraph level formatting.

1. Select the text to be formatted.

2. Either choose "Paragraph" from the Format menu, or click your right Mouse button somewhere within the document window:

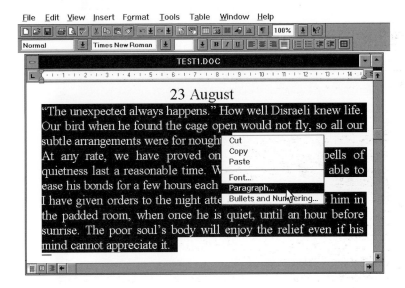

3. Select "Paragraph" from the pop-up menu.

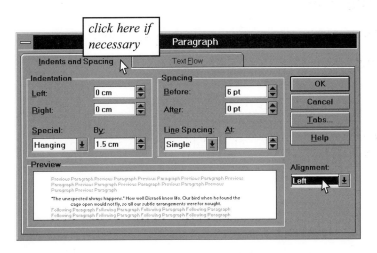

The Indents and Spacing Tab from the Paragraph dialog box

4.   Experiment with the different paragraph controls, checking
      the results in the preview image.

You can adjust the left and right indent, the space above and
below a paragraph, or the line spacing within a paragraph.

In the following example, we set a (vertical) "space before" of 6
points, and a special hanging indent of 1.5cm:

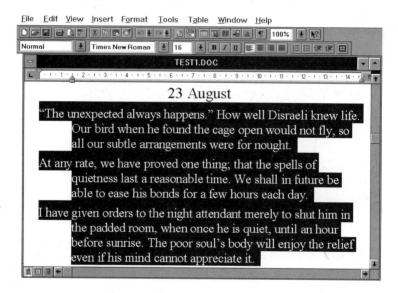

The Points System of Measurement

This system was introduced firstly in the USA last century, and
then adopted by the UK and some European countries.

It provides a standard way of measuring the size of type, and
often refers to the vertical dimension of characters in a given
font. For this reason it is often useful to adjust vertical spacing
using points, so that the space between paragraphs uses the same
system as the paragraphs themselves.

Another Example

In this case we've set a special first line indent of 1.5cm, and also changed the line spacing to "exactly" 18 points. This means that each line in the selected paragraphs will be given exactly 18 points of vertical space regardless of the size of font:

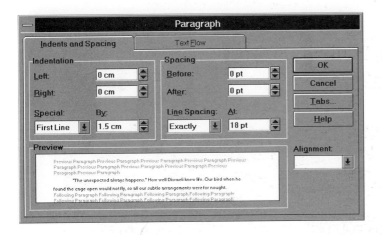

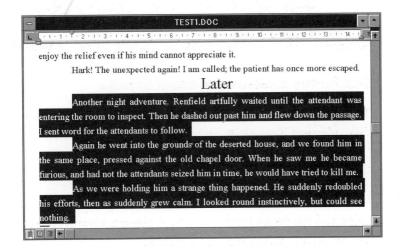

The Textflow Tab

1.   Activate the Paragraph dialog box (either from the Format menu or by clicking in the document window with the right Mouse button).

2.   Choose the TextFlow tab:

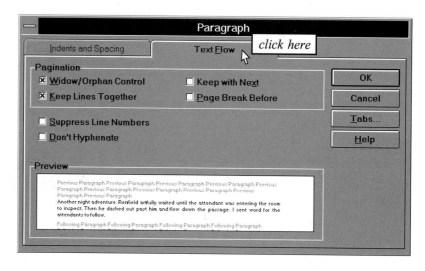

Widow/Orphan Control
If active, Word automatically moves text onto the next page if necessary to prevent Widows and Orphans.

Keep Lines Together
Word will move the text so that the paragraph is not broken over two pages.

Keep With Next
Text is kept with the following paragraph, and not broken over two pages.

Page Break Before
Forces a new page at the start of the paragraph.

Suppress Line Numbers
Switches off numbering for this paragraph if line numbers have been used, renumbering the surrounding paragraphs if necessary.

Don't Hyphenate
Deactivates hyphenation.

CHAPTER

5

Working with a Document

in easy Steps

email

mavis.alexa@virgin.net

User ID.   cracknell136 . /mavander

Password

Scrolling

When your text is too large for the document window, you'll need to use one of the following navigation methods:

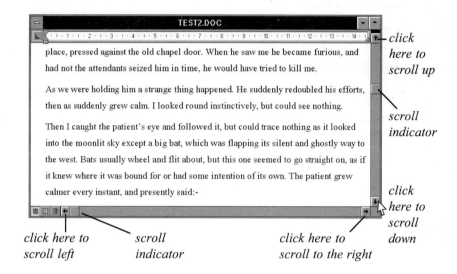

click here to scroll up

scroll indicator

click here to scroll down

click here to scroll left

scroll indicator

click here to scroll to the right

The scroll indicator boxes let you know where you are in a document. For example, when the vertical scroll box is right at the top of the scroll bar, then you are looking at the top (the beginning) of the document.

As you scroll down, this box moves like a lift through a lift shaft.

Quick Ways to Scroll

• Drag the scroll indicator box directly to a new position.

• Click in the scroll bar to either side of the indicator box. The document will scroll in that direction one screen at a time.

• As you move your insertion point, Word will scroll automatically so that it can always be seen in the document window.

Zooming

You can use the Zoom pop-up menu to control the level of
magnification used by the document window.

1.   Either choose an option from the pop-up menu or enter a
      new percentage value between 10 and 200.

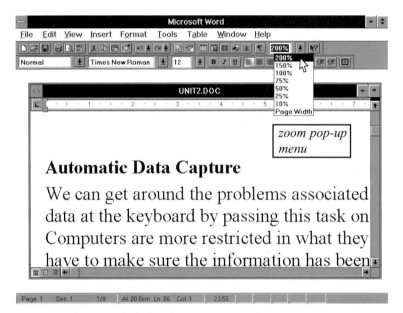

zoom pop-up menu

2.   The Page Width option automatically zooms in or out so
      that the entire width of the page is displayed.

3.   In Page Layout view there are options to display one or
      more entire pages at a time.

Remember that the more you magnify the page, the more you'll
need to scroll. Always try to view the entire horizontal line of
text, since frequent horizontal scrolling can be tedious.

TIP

*If you can afford the space on screen, always maximise both the document
window and the Word window itself by clicking on the Maximise button in
the top right corner of each.*

Maximise button

*This symbol
indicates that the
window is already
Maximised*

The Rulers

The ruler gives you a visual account of the tabs and indents used for any selected text.

1. If the ruler is not visible, activate it by choosing "Ruler" from the View menu.

2. Select one or more paragraphs of text. Experiment by moving the indent markers:

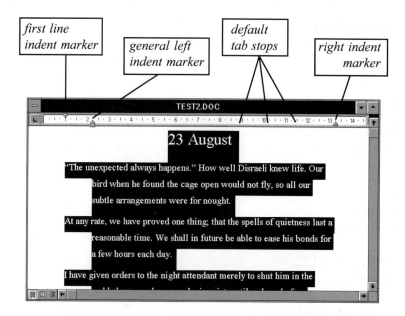

TIP

There is a small square block directly underneath the left indent marker.

Dragging this will move both the left and first line indent markers together.

NOTE

You can also access these controls numerically from the Paragraph dialog box.

Normal and Page Layout View

You can switch between these either via the View menu, or by clicking on the View icons at the bottom left of the screen.

Normal View

This gives a preview of most text effects and some graphic effects. Screen redraw is fast, so this is the best view for most text editing.

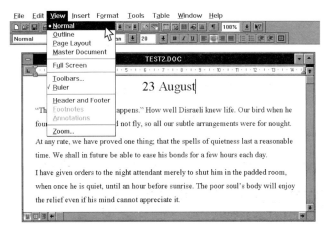

Page Layout View

This previews text and graphic effects, whilst still allowing full editing facilities.

Note the extra options in the Zoom pop-up menu.

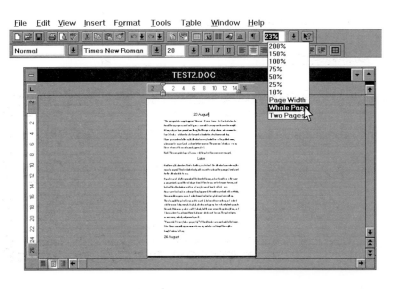

Cut and Paste

1. Select the text to be moved.

2. Holding down the right Mouse button, choose "Cut".

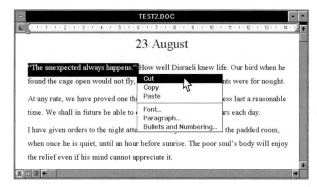

The text is removed and put into the Windows Clipboard.

3. Next position the Insertion point at the destination.
    Holding down the right Mouse button, choose "Paste".

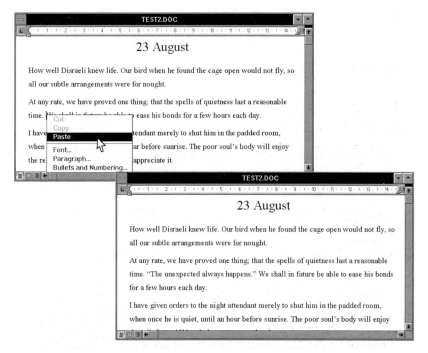

NOTE

You can also Cut and Paste using the Edit menu, or the keyboard shortcuts Control+X, Control+V respectively.

Copy and Paste

1.   Select the text to be copied.

2.   Holding down the right Mouse button, choose "Copy".

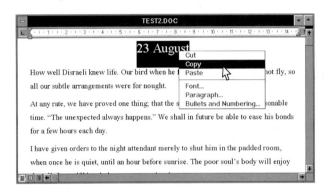

The text is copied into the Windows Clipboard.

3.   Next position the Insertion point at the destination.
      Holding down the right Mouse button, choose "Paste".

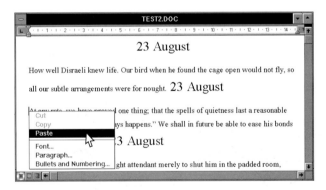

Quick Move

The quickest way to move text is to select it, then drag (from
anywhere within the selected area) directly to the new position.

Quick Copy

If you drag the selected area with the Control key held down,
then the text will be copied to the new position.

Undo and Redo

- Click the Undo button or type Control + Z to undo the last action.

- Alternatively, open the Undo pop-up menu to review and undo more than one action:

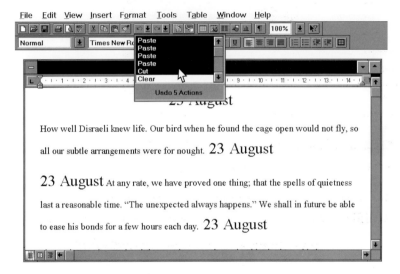

- To redo the undone actions, type Control + Y or use the Redo pop-up menu.

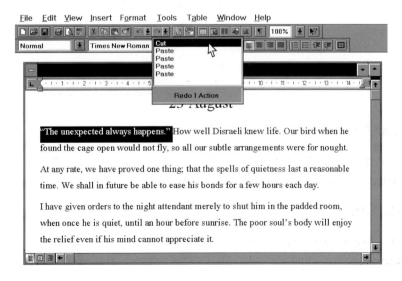

The Format Painter

*The Format
Painter icon*

This allows you to copy the formatting options from one piece of
text to another:

1.   Select the source text and click on the Format Painter icon.

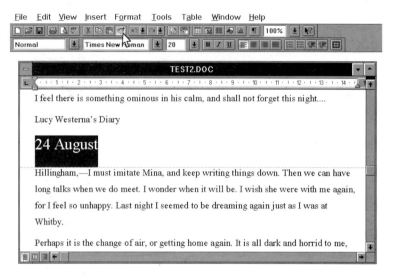

*To copy format to
more than one
destination,
simply double-
click the Format
Painter icon.*

*You can then
apply the new
formatting to as
many pieces of
text as you wish.*

*When you've
finished, either
click back on the
icon or press the
Escape key.*

2.   Now drag across the destination text. The formatting is
     applied to the new text.

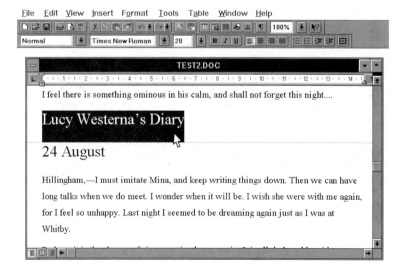

Page Breaks

Word automatically calculates the position of page breaks. These appear in the document window as a dotted horizontal line (a "soft" page break).

To force a Page break, choose "Break" from the Insert menu.

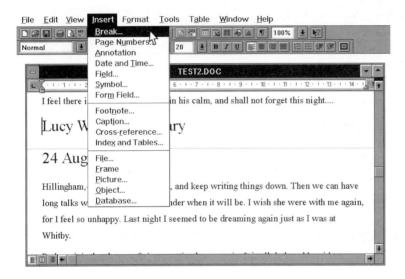

The following dialog box appears. Make sure that "Page Break" is selected and click "OK".

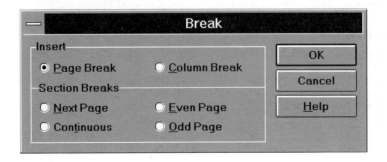

A "Hard" page break is inserted. The result appears as follows:

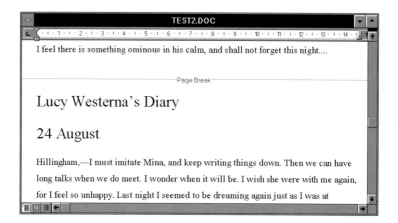

Useful Keyboard Navigation Commands

Cursor keys	Up/down/left/right one space
Control + left/right	Previous/next word
Control + up/down	Previous/next paragraph
Home/End	Beginning/end of line
Control + Home/End	Beginning/end of document
PgUp/PgDn	Move up/down one screen
Control + PgUp/PgDn	Move to top/bottom of window

HINT

If you hold down Shift while making a move, all the text between the old and the new position will be selected.

CHAPTER

6

Rulers and Tabulation

THIS CHAPTER COVERS

In easy Steps

Displaying ¶

There are various special characters such as spaces, carriage returns and tabs which, though normally invisible, all have an important effect on the document.

If you click on the ¶ button in the Toolbar, the display will indicate where these characters are:

The show/hide ¶ icon

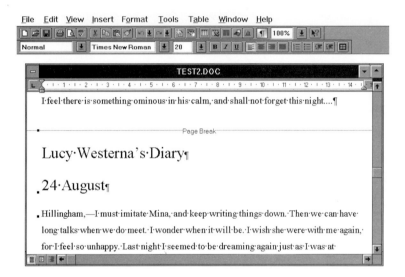

Spaces are shown as single dots (higher up than full stops), paragraph markers as ¶, and tab stops as right pointing arrows.

Other hidden text such as field codes will also be displayed. You will see examples of this later on.

Default Tabulation

WARNING

*Do not feel
tempted to space
out text by
pressing the
Spacebar lots of
times. This will
not produce
consistent results
– use tabulation
instead.*

The default tab stops are set every half inch.

To see how this works:

1. Make sure that the ¶ button is active.

2. Enter items of text separated by a single Tab character.

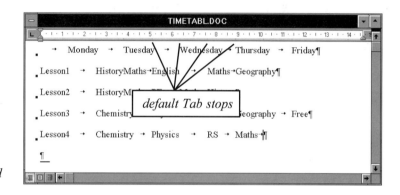

NOTE

*When you press
the Tab key, Word
automatically
moves across the
page, stopping
when it reaches
the next Tab stop
position.*

Creating your own Tabulation

1. Select the text.

2. Click in the ruler to create a new Tab (shaped like an "L") and drag to adjust its position.

TIP

*If you hold down
the ALT key while
dragging a Tab,
the ruler will
display the
distances between
Tab stops.*

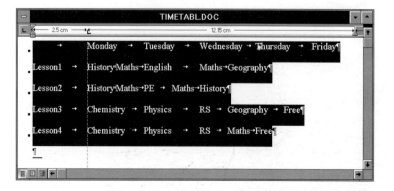

◁

3.   Repeat this process to create more Tab stops.

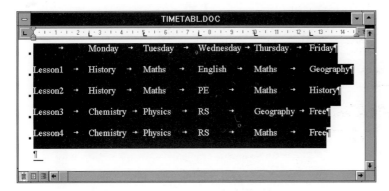

NOTE

Any Tab Stops you create will automatically override the default Tabs.

Deleting Tabs

You can delete your Tab Stops simply by dragging them downwards out of the Ruler.

Different Types of Tab

So far we've created Left Aligned Tabs, which cause text to align along its left edge under the Tab Stop.

WARNING

You can move your own Tab Stops at any time by dragging them within the Ruler - but be sure to select the text first.

1.   Click the Tab Alignment button to change to Centre Tabs.

2.   You can now create centred tabs by clicking in the Ruler:

Tab Alignment button now showing Centred Tabs

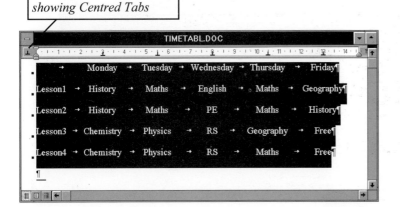

As you click on the Tab Alignment button, it cycles between Left, Centre, Right and Decimal Alignment.

Here is an example of Right Aligned Tabs:

NOTE

Tabulation is a Paragraph level attribute. Each paragraph can have its own Tab Stops, if necessary.

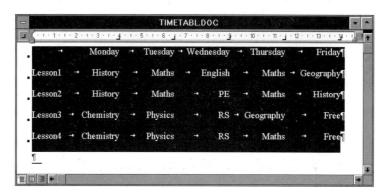

Decimal Tabs are used to line up numbers along the decimal point:

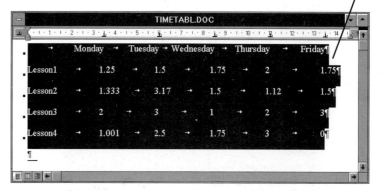

Usually a mixture of different Tabs is required:

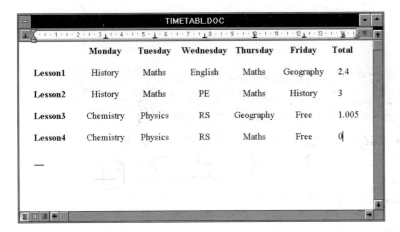

The Tabs Dialog Box

More options can be found in the Tabs dialog box.

1.   Choose "Tabs" from the Format menu.

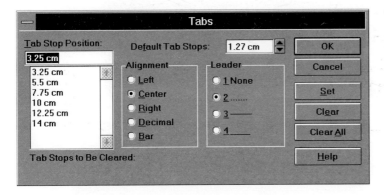

2.   Set the position and alignment of the Tab. The following
      example also uses a Leader consisting of a row of dots...

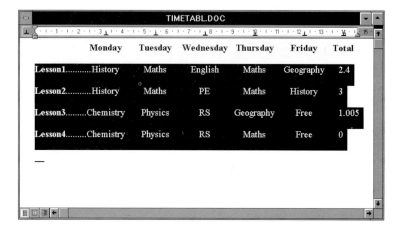

NOTE

You can also access the Tabs dialog via the Paragraph dialog.

Bar Tabs

These can only be accessed from the Tabs dialog box:

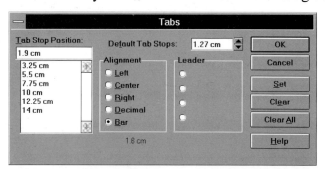

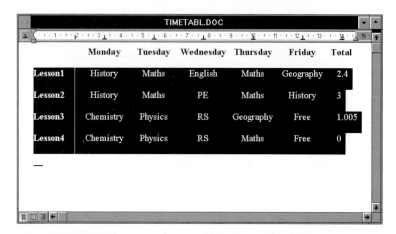

CHAPTER

7

Structured Text

Bullet Text

1. Select the text to be bulleted.

2. Choose "Bullets and Numbering" from the Format menu.

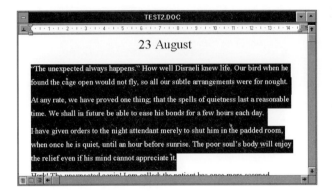

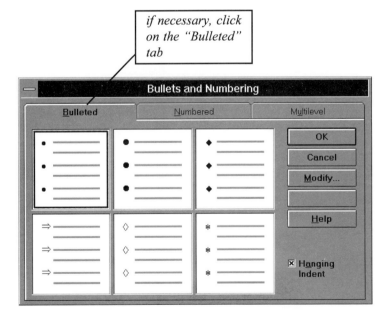

if necessary, click on the "Bulleted" tab

TIP

You can also select "Bullets and Numbering" from the pop-up menu which appears when you click in the document window with the right Mouse button.

3. Choose the type of bullet text. Click on "Modify" to see further options...

The following dialog box appears:

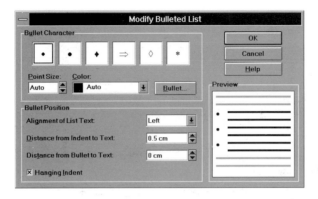

4.   Choose the required settings. Click on the "Bullet" button
      to select from the complete range of characters:

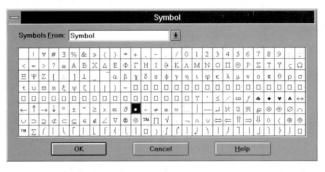

5.
Select the
font and
character.
Click "OK"
to exit all
dialogs.

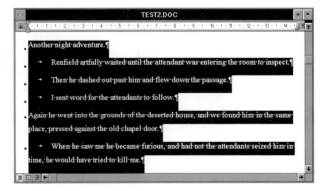

Numbered Text

1.   Select the text to be numbered.

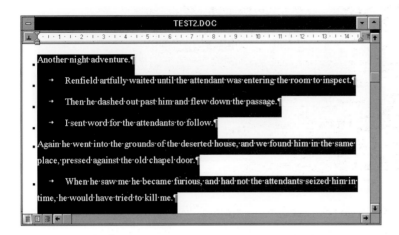

2.   Holding down the right Mouse button, choose "Bullets and Numbering" from the pop-up menu.

3.   If necessary, select the "Numbered" tab.

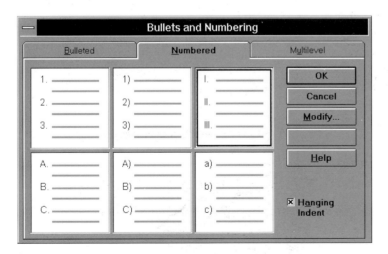

4.   Choose a numbering style. Click on the "Modify" button...

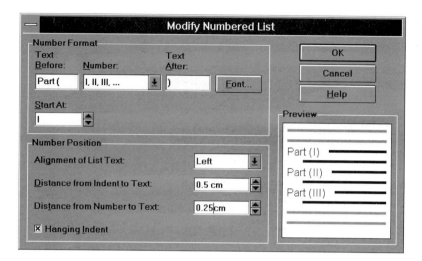

5.   Experiment with different settings, referring to the preview box to see the results.

6.   Click "OK" to exit all dialog boxes.

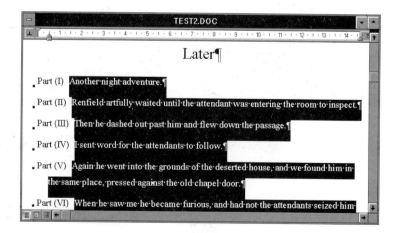

Multilevel Lists

Select the text, choose "Bullets and Numbering" as before, and activate the "Multilevel" tab.

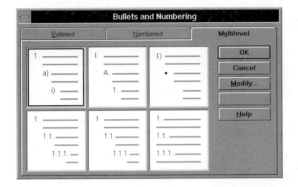

Either choose from the list of standard settings...

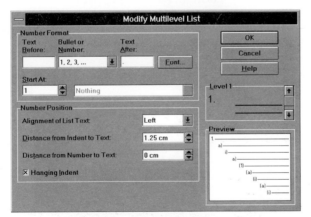

...or use the "Modify" button to customise the list format.

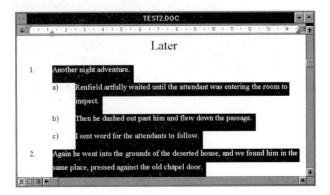

Headers and Footers

Headers normally appear at the top of every page (an example is the text "Word 6 For Windows in Easy Steps" at the top of this page).

Footers can appear at the bottom of each page.

Creating/Modifying a Header

1.   Choose "Header and Footer" from the View menu.

Word will automatically change to Page Layout View. The main page text will be greyed out to let you concentrate on the header.

The Header and Footer Toolbar will also appear.

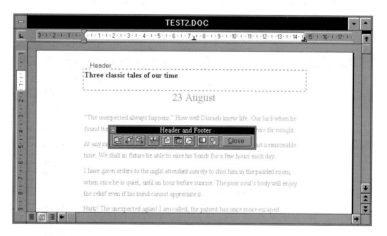

2.   Enter the text and apply formatting as required.

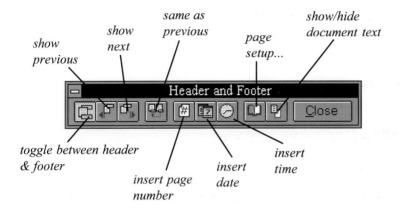

Creating/Modifying a Footer

3. Click on the leftmost button in the Header and Footer toolbar. This will take you to the footer text.

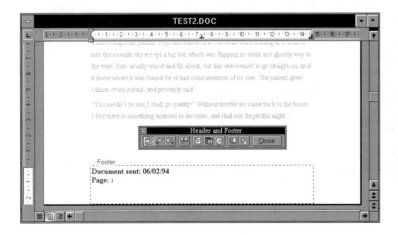

4. Enter the Footer text. You can include automatic page numbers, or the current date or time by clicking on the relevant button in the toolbar.

5. Click "Close" when you've finished.

Now the Header and Footer text is greyed out, and you can edit the main text again.

Note that the picture below shows Page Layout view, in Normal view Headers and Footers do not appear at all.

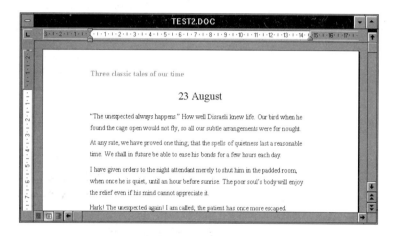

NOTE

By default, the Header and Footer on a page will apply to all remaining pages in the document. You can override this by editing the Headers/Footers for other pages separately.

CHAPTER

8

Automatic Features

in easy steps

Find

Word can be instructed to search through your document for
particular words, groups of characters, or formatting attributes.

1.   Choose "Find" from the Edit menu (or type Control + F)

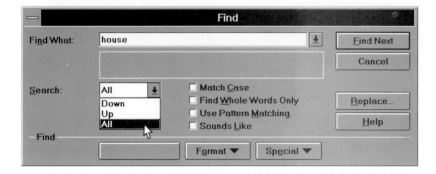

TIP

*You can set the
Find dialog to
look for text in
particular case,
for whole words
(rather than
groups of letters),
to use wildcard
searching, or
phonetic
matching.*

2.   Enter your search text in the "Find What" box.

3.   Set the search direction, either from the Insertion Point
     downwards, upwards or throughout the entire document.

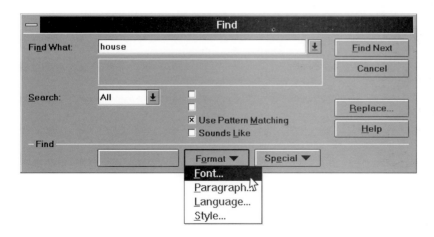

4.   If you want to make a search based on attributes, open the
     Format pop-up menu, and choose the relevant option.

In this example we're searching for TimesNewRoman 14 point
text:

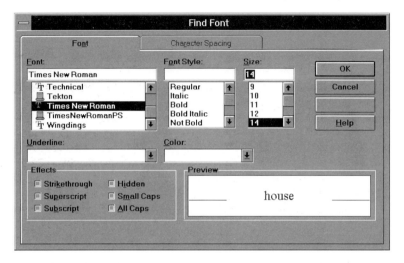

5.   Click "OK" to return to the Find dialog, then click on the
      Find button to start the search.

Word highlights the first instance of text matching your search
criteria:

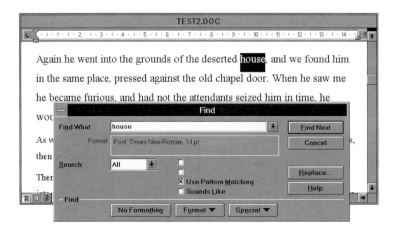

Click on Find Next to continue searching for subsequent
instances of text that match the same search criteria.

Replace

This works in the same way as Find, but with additional facilities for automatically substituting new text and/or formatting.

1.   Choose Replace from the Edit menu (or type Control + H).

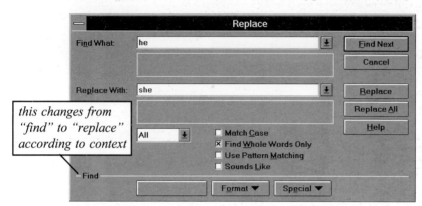

this changes from "find" to "replace" according to context

TIP

There is a button in the Find dialog which takes you directly to the Replace dialog.

2.   Enter the "Find" text, then use the Format pop-up menu to set any text attributes.

3.   Enter the "Replace with" text. Note that, as soon as you click in the "Replace with" box, the lower section of the dialog box switches from "Find" to "Replace". You can now set the Replace attributes, if necessary.

Special Characters

You can use the "Special" pop-up menu in the Replace dialog box to easily insert the keyboard codes for special characters. In this example we're looking for two consecutive line breaks, and replacing with a single line break.

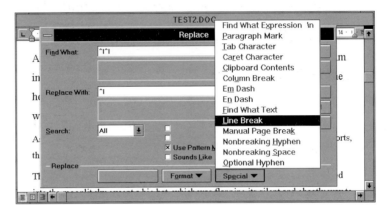

The Special Pop-up Menu

These special codes act like wildcards, allowing Word to find text which varies according to some structure.

<table>
<tr><td></td><td>Find Wildcards</td><td>Replace Codes</td></tr>
<tr><td>^?</td><td>Any character</td><td>^&</td><td>Re-insert the "Find What" text (see example in margin).</td></tr>
<tr><td>^#</td><td>Any digit</td><td>^0nnn</td><td>ANSII or ASCII character</td></tr>
<tr><td>^$</td><td>Any letter</td><td>^c</td><td>Clipboard contents</td></tr>
<tr><td>^w</td><td>White space</td><td></td><td></td></tr>
</table>

"Find What" example

If you entered the text:
MS Windows
in the Find box, and then:
^& for Workgroups
under Replace, then all instances of "MS Windows" would change to "MS Windows for Workgroups".

For example, if "Find Whole Words Only" was active, entering 19^#^# in the "Find" box, would instruct Word to locate any instances of the characters "19" followed by two digits. So it would locate "1901" and "1999" but not "1899" or "19101".

Pattern Matching

If you activate "Pattern matching" in the Find or Replace dialog, you can set up more sophisticated searches.

A Simple Example

Typing "[a-g]" will now indicate any character in the range "a" through to "g", so entering "196[4-9]" would match with "1964", "1965", "1966", "1967", "1968" and "1969".

More Complex Search Criteria

When working inside the Find or Replace dialog, press the F1 key and click on "Advanced Search Criteria" for a full list of the options including explanations and examples.

Spell Checking

1. If you don't want to spell check your entire document, then select only the text you require.

2. Choose "Spelling" from the Tools menu, or click on the Spellcheck icon.

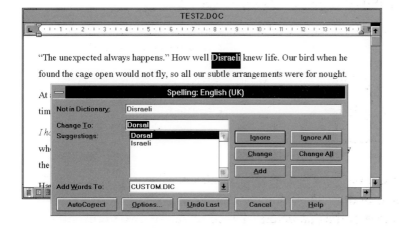

HINT

The shortcut key for Spell Checking is F7.

3.   When a suspect word is found, you can:

This message appears when Word has finished checking through the document.

•   Click "Change" to replace it with Word's suggestion.

•   Select another entry from the list of suggestions, and click "Change".

•   Enter your own correction and click "Change".

•   Click "Ignore" if the word is correct (e.g. a proper noun).

HINT

You can make Word change or ignore all instances of the current text by clicking "Ignore All" or "Change All".

4.   If you enter your own correction and would like the word to be added to the dictionary, click the "Add" button.

5.   You can change dictionary file by selecting from the "Add words to" pop-up menu.

6.   Clicking the "Options" button takes you to the "Spelling" tab of the Options dialog box:

NOTE

You can also access this from the Tools menu.

See Chapter 13, The Spelling Tab for customising dictionaries.

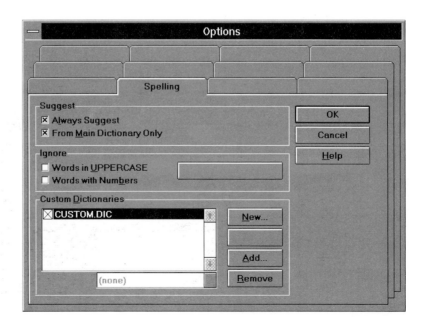

Word Count

1. To count the words in one area only, select it in the normal way, otherwise the entire document will be scanned.

2. Choose "Word Count" from the Tools menu:

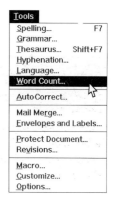

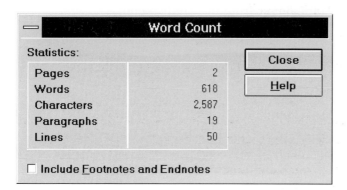

Thesaurus

1. Select the word to be used.

2. Press Shift + F7 or choose "Thesaurus" from the Tools menu:

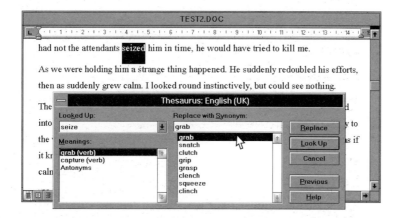

AutoCorrect

Many of us make the same spelling or typing mistakes again and
again. I have a very real problem with the word "occasion".

We can instruct Word to automatically substitute the correction:

1.   Choose AutoCorrect from the Tools menu:

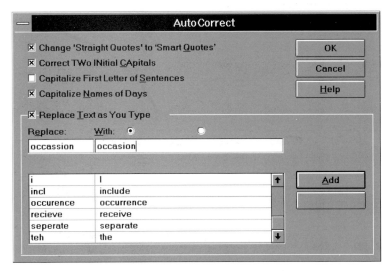

2.   Enter the mistake, the correction, then click on the Add
      button.

3.   Now when you type, Word spots the error and substitutes
      automatically:

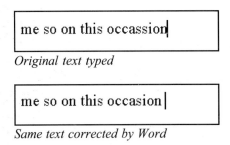

Original text typed

Same text corrected by Word

You can now continue through the rest of your life completely
unaware that you are consistently failing to spell correctly.

AutoText

This is a less automatic version of AutoCorrect, and is useful for setting up your own abbreviations.

If you find that you often need to type the same text, then it would be worth setting up an AutoText entry:

Creating an Autotext Entry

1. Type the text and select.

2. Click on the Edit Autotext button in the Toolbar:

The selected text is automatically inserted into the "Selection" area of the AutoText dialog box.

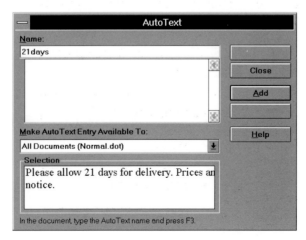

3. Edit the "Name" box to the abbreviation you require. Click "OK".

Using AutoText

1.   Simply type the abbreviation:

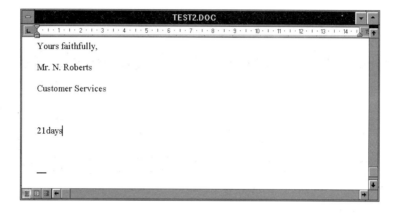

2.   Press F3 or the AutoText icon in the Toolbar.

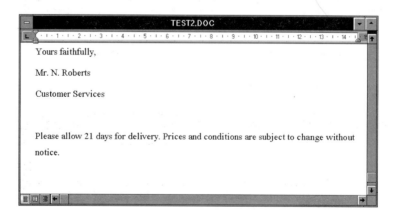

The abbreviation is inflated back into the original text.

The Spike

The Spike is a temporary piece of AutoText which can be added to with a single key command.

Creating a Spike

1. Select some text and press Control + F3 keys.

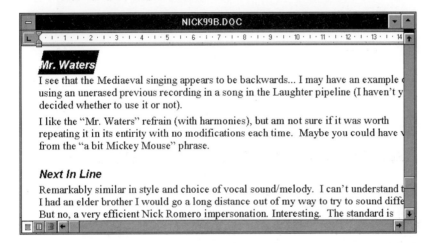

The text disappears. It has been impaled on the Spike.

2. Repeat the process with a second piece of text.

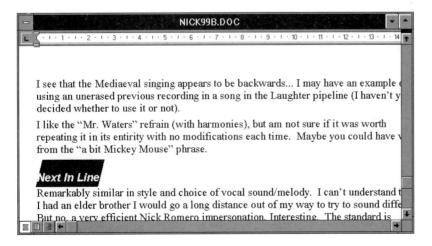

3.   You can repeat this more times if necessary. Each time you
      press Control + F3 any selected text is put onto the Spike.

4.   Finally, place the insertion point at the destination for the
      text:

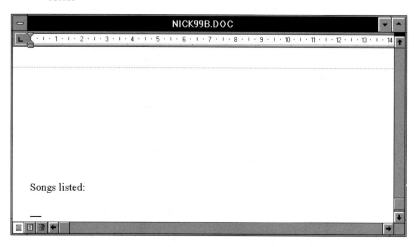

5.   Press Control + Shift + F3 keys.

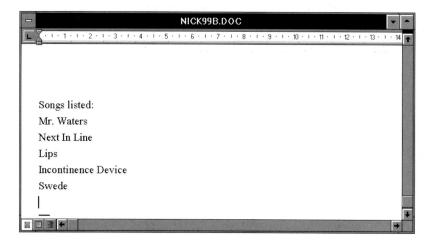

The text is pulled off the spike and placed back into the
document.

Behind the Scenes

When you have text on the Spike, it is actually stored under the AutoText name "Spike".

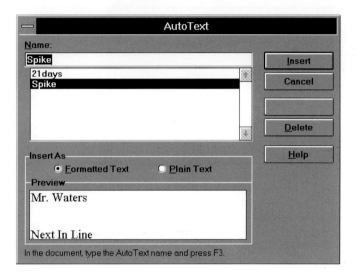

This means that you can place a copy of the Spike (without depleting its contents) either with the AutoText command (in the Edit menu), or by typing "Spike" and pressing F3.

Hyphenation

1.   You can change the hyphenation options for your
      document by choosing "Hyphenation" from the Tools
      menu:

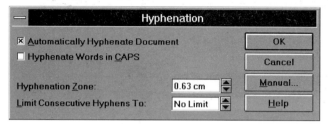

2.   If you click on the "Manual" button you can review
      hyphenation manually throughout your document:

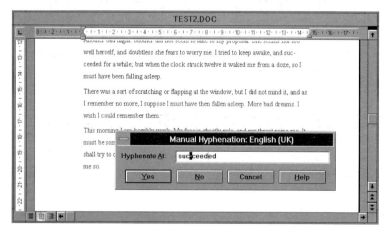

NOTE

*You can also
override
hyphenation for
individual
paragraphs by
clicking on the
"Don't hyphenate"
button in the Text
Flow tab of the
Paragraph dialog
box.*

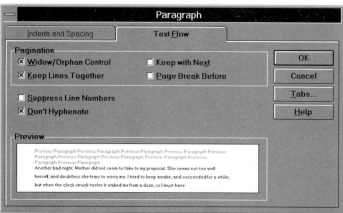

Grammar Checking

1.   Choose "Grammar" from the Tools menu:

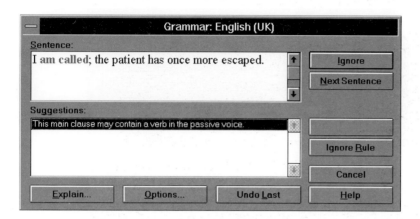

2.   Click the Explain button to find out about the guideline or
      rule you may have broken.

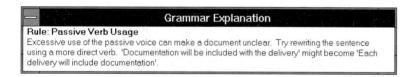

A different approach to grammar is required for different types
of document:

3.   Click on the Options button from the Grammar dialog box.
      If you are currently working in the document then you can
      access this directly by choosing "Options" from the Tools
      menu and then the "Grammar" tab.

The following dialog box appears:

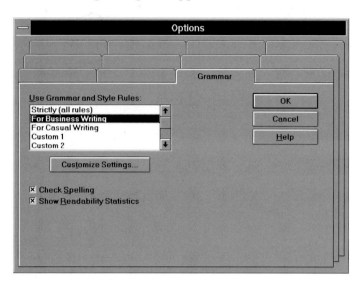

4.   You can tailor the grammar checking to your own
      requirements by clicking on the "Customize Settings"
      button:

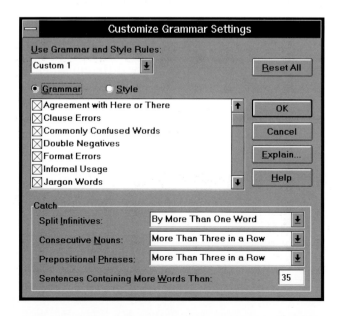

When deciding on what to use, it may be worth clicking on the Explain button to help you determine the usefulness of a rule:

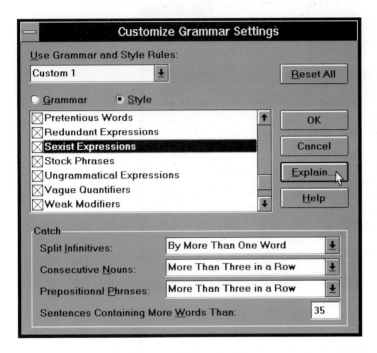

Grammar Explanation

Rule: Sexist Expressions
These rules flag expressions that are likely to be considered sexist or reflective of stereotypes based on gender. The error messages may offer alternatives or suggest rephrasing the sentence to eliminate the expression. For example, one rule will flag sentences like 'Say hello to the little woman', because 'little woman' is considered a sexist expression; it suggests the terms 'wife', 'partner', or 'spouse' as alternatives.

Grammar Explanation

Rule: Pretentious Words
These rules flag unnecessarily complex words and offer simple, straightforward alternatives. The expressions addressed in this rule set are not considered jargon words, since they do not come from a specialised discipline. Like jargon words, however, they may seem affected or pretentious to some readers, and it is often best to replace them with a simpler word or phrase. For example, one rule in this set will flag a sentence like 'This is what usually eventuates in such situations' and suggest replacing 'eventuate' with the simpler expressions 'take place' or 'happen'.

Readability Statistics

When the Grammar Check is over, Word displays the Readability Statistics information:

Unfortunately no one has, as yet, figured out a way of automatically analysing the Boredom level of a document.

This is one job still left to us lucky humans...

Readability Statistics	
Counts:	
Words	651
Characters	2,764
Paragraphs	27
Sentences	45
Averages:	
Sentences per Paragraph	1.7
Words per Sentence	14.5
Characters per Word	4.1
Readability:	
Passive Sentences	4%
Flesch Reading Ease	85.2
Flesch-Kincaid Grade Level	4.4
Coleman-Liau Grade Level	7.4
Bormuth Grade Level	8.9
OK	Help

The Flesch Reading Ease value is in the range 0..100, increasing with ease of reading. Standard text rates between 60 and 70.

The Grade Level values give an indication as to the school grade appropriate for your text. For example, a level of 3 means that it would be understandable by someone in the third grade or below. Standard text normally weighs in between 7 and 8.

CHAPTER

9

Styles

THIS CHAPTER COVERS

In easy steps

Using the Default Styles

A Style is a complete collection of type attributes saved under a single name. There are two main benefits to this:

- Your document will have a visual consistency if, for example, all your subheads look the same.

- You can quickly make drastic but coherent changes to the format of your document by redefining the styles already used by the text.

Applying a Style

1. Select the text.

2. Select a style from the pop-up menu:

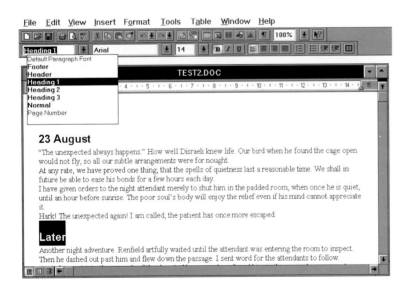

HINT

The keyboard shortcut for this is Control + Shift + S.

Then type the first few letters of the Style and press the down arrow key.

The text has now been set to this Style. Whenever you select text on the page, the pop-up menu will indicate which Style is currently being used.

By default all text starts off using the Style "Normal".

Editing an Existing Style

1.   Select some text in the document which already uses the style to be changed.

2.   Use the Toolbar and menus as normal to experiment with changes in formatting.

3.   When you are happy with the changes, reselect the style from the pop-up list and press Return:

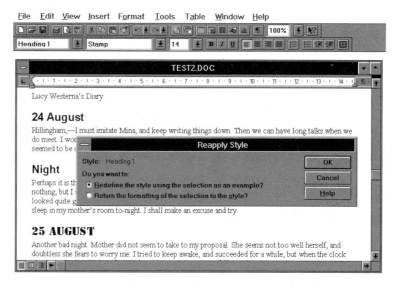

4.   In the dialog which appears, make sure the "Redefine.." option is selected and click "OK".

All text in the document using this style will now change automatically...

Creating a New Style

1. Format the text as normal in the document.

2. When you are happy with its appearance, enter the new style name in the pop-up menu and press Return:

The new style is automatically created, and can now be applied to other text.

Using the Format Painter

The Format Painter icon

You can use the Format Painter to apply the same style to different pieces of text:

1. Highlight some text already using the style.

2. Double click on the Format Painter icon to absorb the text attributes.

3. Select the text to be changed. Repeat this process for each instance.

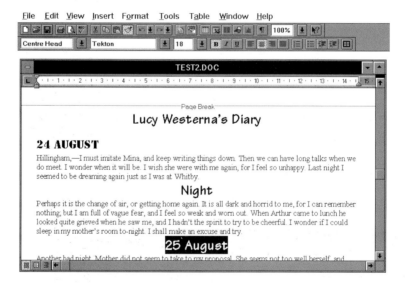

4. When you've finished, click back on the Format Painter to deselect or press the Escape key.

The Style Dialog Box

1. Choose "Style" from the Format menu, alternatively press Control + Shift + S twice (pressing this once takes you to the pop-up menu).

The dialog box which appears lets you preview and manage all the Styles:

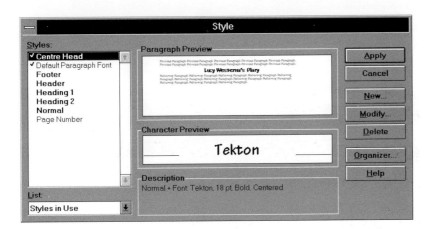

Creating a New Style Using The Dialog Boxes

2. Click on the "New" button:

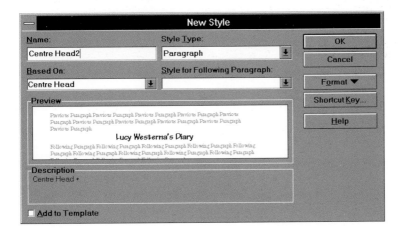

From this dialog you can put together the style definition.

Setting a Keyboard Shortcut for a Style

3.   Click the "Shortcut key" button.

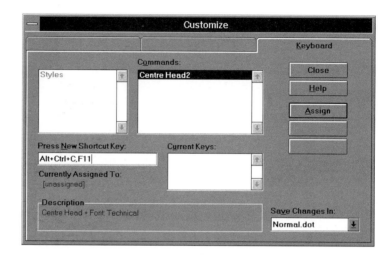

4.   Enter the Shortcut key for the Style and click the "Assign" button. You can repeat this process to add more than one keyboard shortcut for the same Style.

5.   When you have finished, click the "Close" button to return to the previous dialog box.

Setting the Format

6.   Back in the New Style dialog box, select "Font" from the
      "Format" pop-up menu:

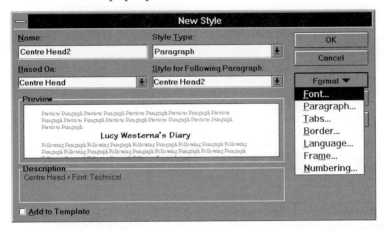

This will take you to the Font dialog box. When you have
finished making the settings you may also want to use the
"Format" pop-up menu to set other attributes such as Paragraph.

7.   Click "OK". The new Style is added to the list.

Modifying a Style

From the Styles dialog box, click on "Modify".

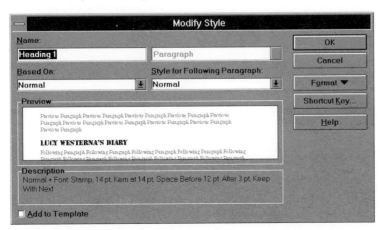

Character Level Styles

Normally Styles operate on a Paragraph level, i.e. they only apply to whole paragraphs.

To create a character level style:

1. Choose "New" from the Style dialog.

2. Select "Character" from "Style Type" pop-up menu:

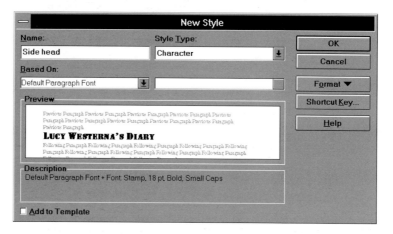

3. Use the "Format" pop-up to set the character level attributes:

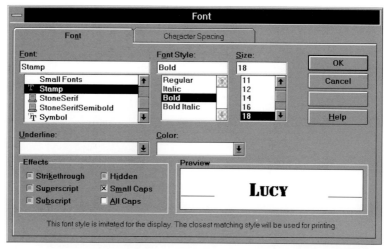

You can now apply your character Style to individual words or phrases without affecting the entire surrounding paragraph.

If text already uses a paragraph Style, then the character Style will override these settings:

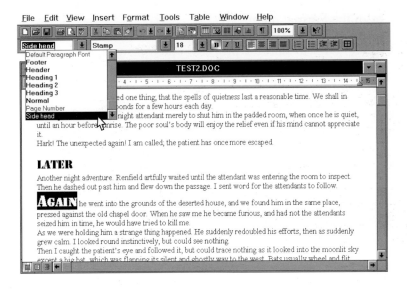

NOTE

Character level Style names appear as normal text in any Style list, whereas Paragraph level Style names are in bold.

AutoFormat

The AutoFormat icon

If you have created a document using no Styles or even ordinary formatting, then AutoFormat can attempt to take care of this for you.

1. Either click on the AutoFormat icon in the Toolbar or, if you want to monitor the changes, choose "AutoFormat" from the Format menu.

2. Click "OK" to start the process. The following dialog will then appear:

3. To manually review and authorise changes, click on the "Review Changes" button.

or

To control the overall look of the document, click on "Style Gallery".

The Style Gallery

1. You can activate the Style Gallery dialog either via the AutoFormat dialog or directly from the Format menu.

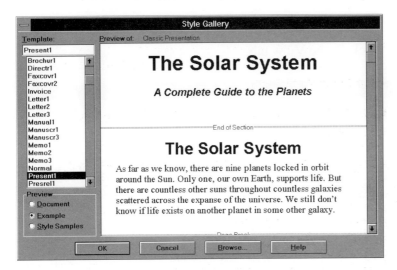

2. Choose a Template design, then a preview option. "Document" shows you how your document would look with the proposed Style definitions. "Example" shows you an example document demonstrating the different styles.

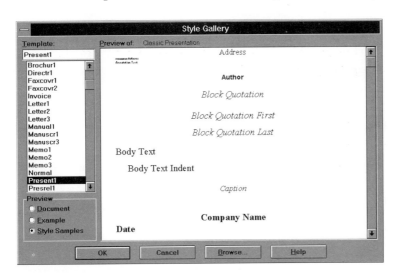

"Samples" lists each style name using its own attributes.

3. Click "OK" if you want your document to adopt the displyed Style definition.

Displaying Style Names

Sometimes it is useful to instantly see which styles are being used by the paragraphs in your document.

1.   Choose "Options" from the Tools menu.

2.   Click on the View tab.

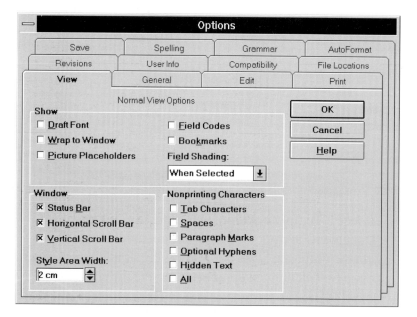

3.   Set the "Style Area Width" to a figure greater than zero.

In this example we've used a 2cm margin area in which to list the Styles used.

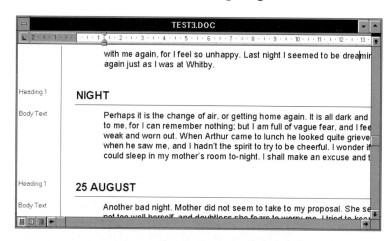

CHAPTER

10

Templates

Using Templates

A Template contains a range of settings to be used as a starting point for a new document.

The Normal Template

1.   Choose "New" from the File menu:

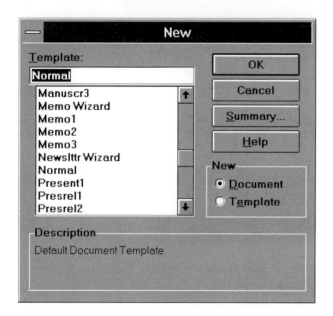

Word lists the templates available. Often you'll use the "Normal" template.

2.   Leave the option as "Normal" and click "OK".

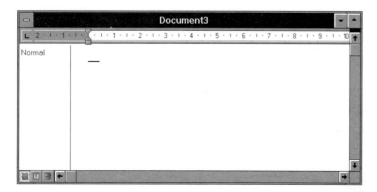

NOTE

If you use the "New" icon instead of the File menu, Word uses the "Normal" template.

Behind the Scenes...

*The Normal Template is stored as the file **NORMAL.DOT** within Word's Templates directory.*

Form Templates

1.   Choose "New" from the File menu.

2.   Select the "Weektime" Template. Click "OK".

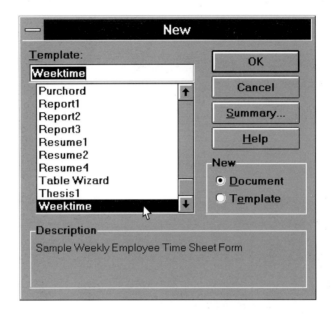

Form Filling

"Weektime" contains a complete design for a weekly time sheet form. Forms normally contain fields, which can be easily filled in or edited without disturbing the surrounding text.

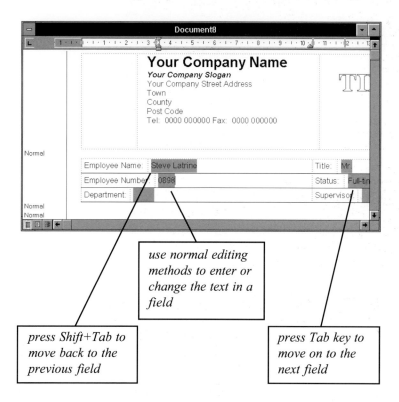

Note that most of the menu options are greyed out, and that you cannot edit the main text in the document. You're restricted to editing the fields, saving and printing.

Provided the template is set exactly the way you want, this allows you to easily produce forms without being distracted by Word's vast array of features and controls.

Changing the Form

1.   Go to the Tools menu and choose "Unprotect Document".

2.   You can now fully edit the document, adapting it to your own ends:

For more information about creating this type of document, see chapter 18 "Forms".

Changing Template Defaults

Defaults are settings which are used initially when you create a
new document or add new text.

1. Open the Font dialog box.

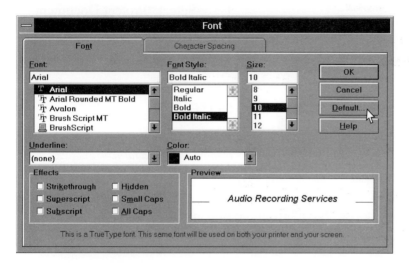

2. Choose your required settings and then click on the
    "Default" button.

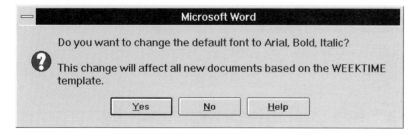

3. If you click "Yes", the font information will be saved into
    the currently used Template document.

Setting Up a New Template

Any document can be saved as a Template, but in this example we'll return to our form from earlier on.

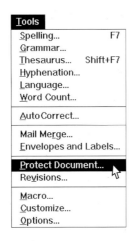

1. Select "Protect Document" from the Tools menu.

2. Set the Protect option to "Forms".

NOTE

We only need to do this if the template is to be used as a form.

3. Choose "Save" from the File menu:

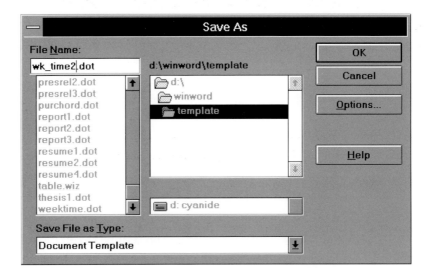

4. Choose "Document Template" as the File Type.

The document will automatically be saved with a .DOT extension within Word's Template directory.

Changing Styles in a Template

When you open a document, Word uses the Styles built into the Template selected.

As we saw earlier, you can alter these Styles for individual documents using the "Style" command from the Format menu.

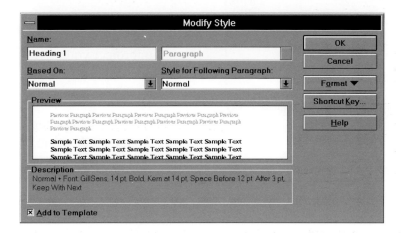

To copy a style change back into the Template itself, click on "Add to Template" in the Modify Style dialog box.

NOTE

*If you record a Style modification to the "Normal" template, this will be stored in **NORMAL.DOT** and hence affect most new documents.*

The Templates & Add-ins Dialog

Word always keeps track of the Template used to create a
document. It is possible to change this even after you've started
work:

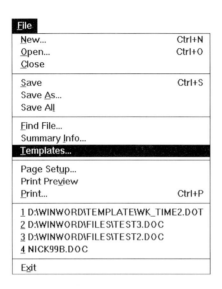

1. If necessary,
    unprotect your
    document (Tools
    menu).

2. Choose "Templates"
    from the File menu.

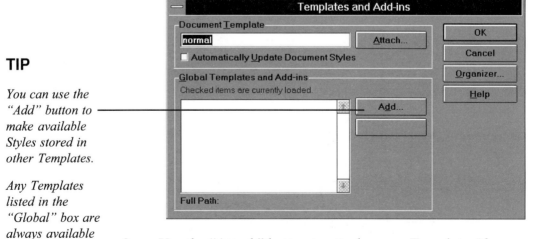

TIP

*You can use the
"Add" button to
make available
Styles stored in
other Templates.*

*Any Templates
listed in the
"Global" box are
always available
(these are kept in
Word's STARTUP
directory).*

3. Use the "Attach" button to attach a new Template. If you
    select "Automatically Update Document Styles" then the
    Styles from the new Template will be re-applied to the
    document text.

CHAPTER

11

The Organizer

The Organizer Dialog Box

The Organizer allows you to easily copy information from one
Word file to another.

1.   Choose "Templates" from the File menu.

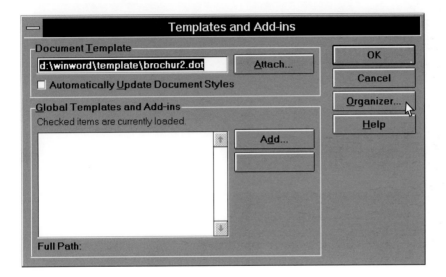

2.   Click on the "Organizer" button.

NOTE

*You may need to Unprotect a document (Tools menu) before the Organiser
can copy information into it.*

The AutoText Tab

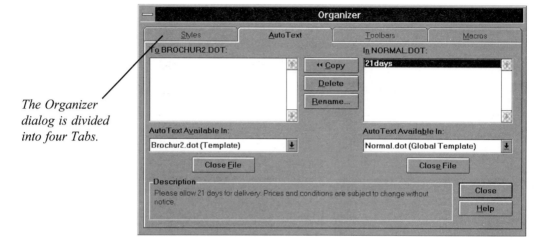

The Organizer dialog is divided into four Tabs.

3.   Using the AutoText Tab you can copy AutoText entries from one document to another.

NOTE

If an AutoText entry is copied into a Global Template, NORMAL.DOT for example, then it will be available to all documents.

The Styles Tab

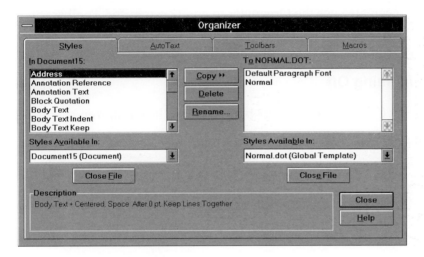

4. The Styles Tab allows you to copy styles freely from one file to another.

NOTE

If a Style is copied into a Global Template like NORMAL.DOT, it will then be available to all documents.

Toolbars and Macros

You can also use the Organizer to copy customised Toolbars and Macros from one file to another. Examples of these can be found in Chapter 24 "Customising Word".

Finishing Off

5.   Click on the "Close" button to exit the Organizer.

6.   Click "Yes" to save the changes.

Summary Info

Standard DOS filenames, with their eight-character limitation and rejection of special symbols, provide a document reference system which is rather less than ideal.

1. Go to the File menu and choose "Summary Info".

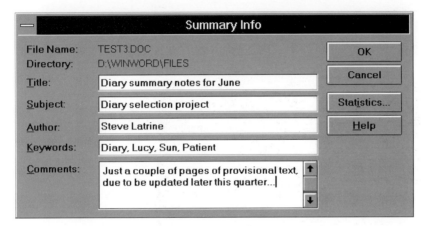

2. Enter the relevant details. Word will be able to locate files on the basis of this text.

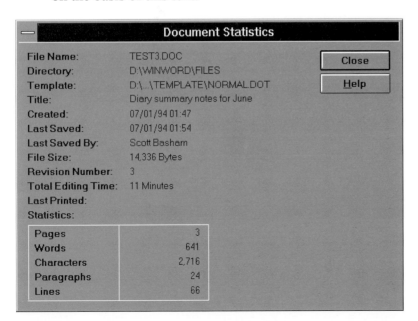

NOTE

A document statistics information box can be brought up from the Summary Info dialog box.

Find File

This utility allows you to efficiently locate and organise both Word documents and other files.

1.   Choose "Find file" from the File menu.

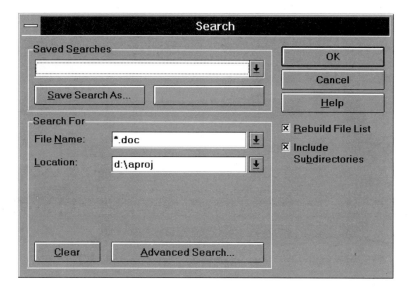

The Search dialog box appears.

2.   Enter your search criteria and click "OK".

The Find File dialog box appears:

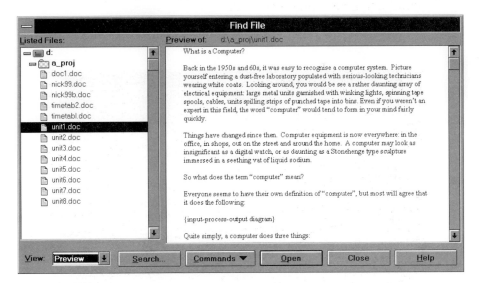

3.   Ensure that Preview is selected from the View pull-down
menu.

Find File will show a preview on the right of any selected file.

The Commands Submenu

Use this pop-up menu to perform
actions on the file(s) selected.

Advanced Searches

4.   Click on "Search" to get back to the Search dialog, then
      click on "Advanced Search".

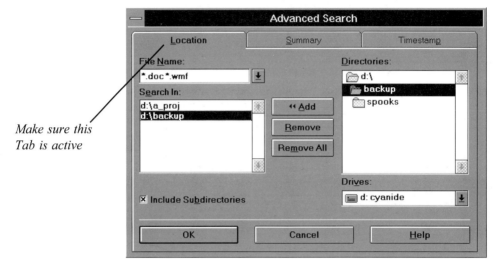

Make sure this Tab is active

Using the Location Tab you can build up a list of disks and
directories to be searched.

5.   Locate the required disk directory in the Directories box
      and click "Add".

6.   Repeat this until all the required directories have been
      inserted in the list.

NOTE

•   You can also remove single items by selecting and then
      clicking on the "Remove" button.

•   To clear the list completely (allowing you to start again),
      click on "Remove All".

7.   Click on the Summary Tab.

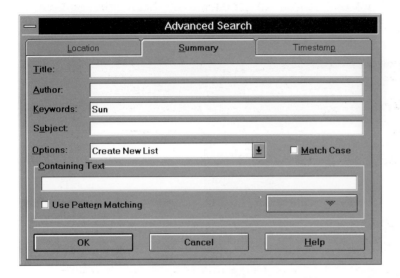

8.   Enter the search criteria for the files' Summary Info.

9.   Finally, click on the Timestamp Tab.

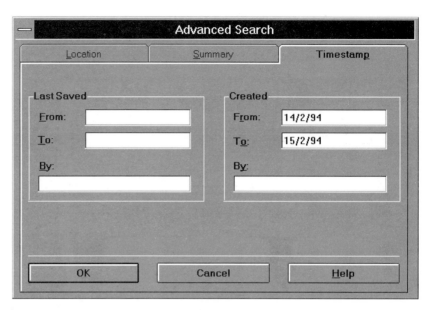

10.   Enter the range of date or time values attributed to the
      files. You can base this on when the file was created, when
      it was saved, or a combination of the two.

11.   Finally, click "OK" to return to the Search dialog box.

Saving your Search Settings

12.   To save the search criteria click on "Save Search As":

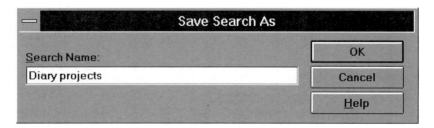

13.   Enter a name for the search and click "OK".

14.   This search will now be available in the Saved Searches
      pop-up list.

CHAPTER

12

Wizards

Wizards

Wizard documents are 'alive'; they actually build and design themselves. They do this by asking you a series of questions when you create a new file based on a Wizard Template.

An example

1. Go to the File menu and choose "New".

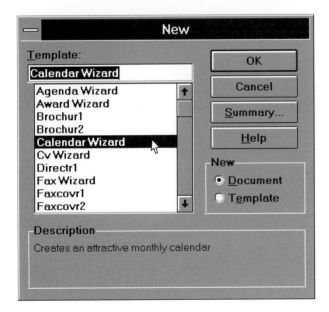

2. Select the Template "Calendar Wizard" and click "OK".

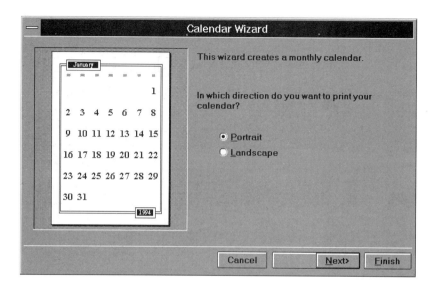

3.   Select Landscape orientation and click the "Next" button.

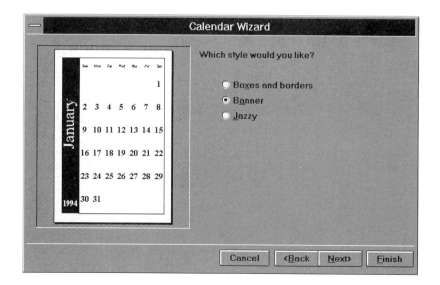

4.   Select the "Banner" style and click on "Next".

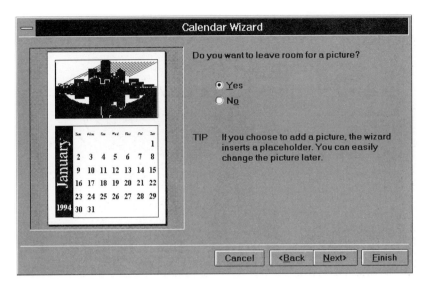

5.   Select "Yes" to include a picture and click "Next".

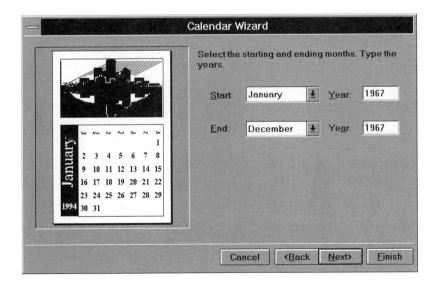

6.   Enter the range of dates and click "Next".

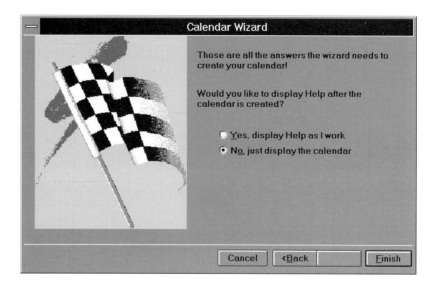

7.   Select "No" to display just the calendar without help text.

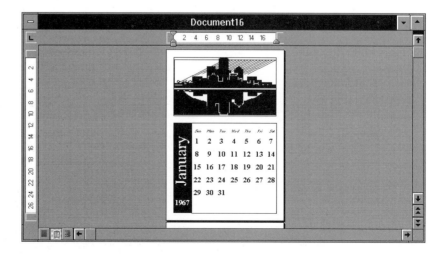

You now have a complete calendar document ready for editing,
saving and printing.

CHAPTER

13

The Options
Dialog Box

The Options dialog box covers 12 different categories. Rather than cram all the functions into one screen, this dialog is one of many which uses Tabs to organise the controls.

To select the category you desire, simply click on the appropriate Tab at the top of the dialog box.

The View Tab

1.	Choose "Options" from the Tools menu.

2.	Make sure the View tab is active:

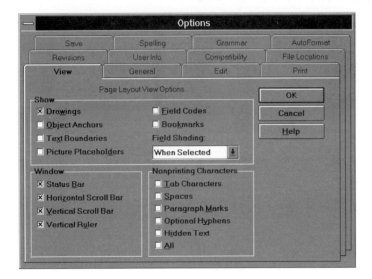

3.	Select the items to be displayed in your current view.

NOTE

The options displayed will vary depending on whether you are currently using Normal, Page Layout or Outline view.

4.	Exit from the dialog box, change to a different View, then choose Options again.

The dialog box has changed.

The General Tab

5.   Make sure the General tab is active.

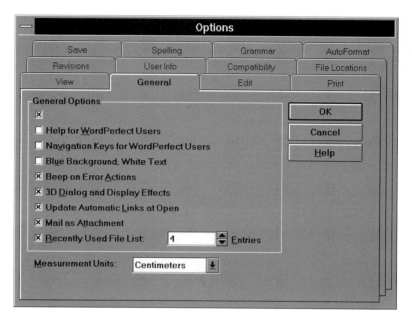

From here you can set general operating preferences for Word.

In particular:

•   You can set the Measurement units to inches, centimetres, points or picas.

•   The WordPerfect help will illustrate the Word equivalent of WordPerfect commands. You can also set the navigation keys to work as they do in WordPerfect.

The Edit Tab

6. Activate the Edit tab.

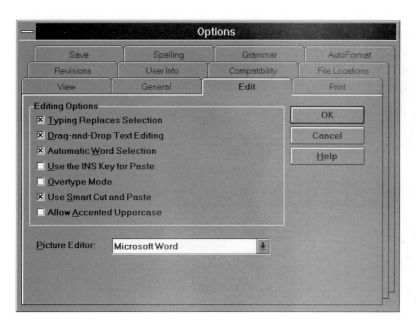

From here you can set the Edit preferences. In particular:

*   "Typing Replaces Selection" means that any text you have selected will be replaced by any new text typed.

*   "Drag-and-Drop" Editing allows you to move selected text by dragging, and to copy selected text by dragging while pressing the Control key.

*   The Overtype option can more easily be activated and deactivated by pressing the INS key (provided it isn't being used for the Paste command) during editing.

*   Smart Cut and Paste removes white space when using the Clipboard.

The Print Tab

7.   Make sure the Print tab is active.

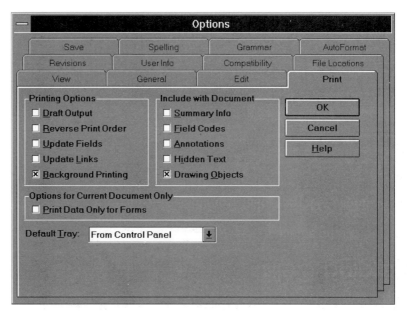

From here you can set the printing options.

For example:

*   You can choose which aspects of a document to print.

*   You can set Word to update any items linked to external files at the time of printing.

*   There are two forms of output: Draft is faster, but of lower quality.

NOTE

This tab can be accessed directly from the Print dialog box.

The Revisions Tab

8.   Activate the Revisions tab.

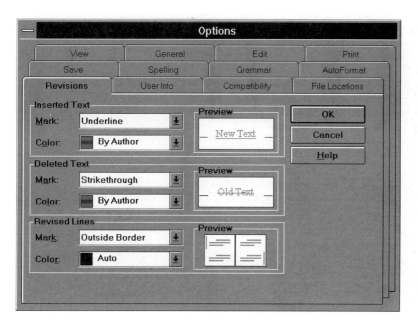

The revisions feature allows Word to keep a visual record of changes (revisions) made to a saved document.

From this dialog you can choose the conventions to be used for displaying inserted, deleted and revised text. The preview boxes give you an indication as to how this will work.

The User Info Tab

9.   Make sure the User Info tab is active.

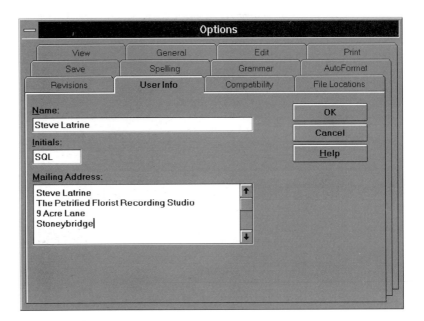

Use this dialog to record information about yourself. This is used by features such as Envelope and Summary Info.

The Compatibility Tab

10.   Click on the Compatibility tab.

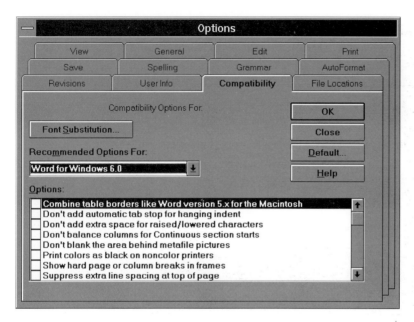

From here you can specify how you want Word to deal with documents created in other Word Processors or earlier versions of Word itself.

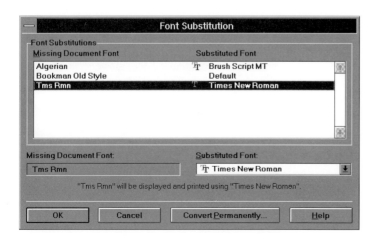

Font Substitution

Word will automatically select a substitute for a font used by the document but missing from your system.

The File Locations Tab

11.   Make sure the File Locations tab is active.

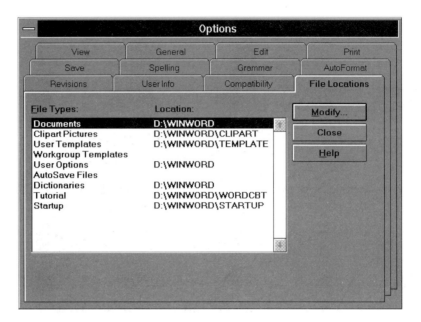

Use this dialog to locate the directories used by Word for various files.

For example the **STARTUP** directory contains all Templates set for global use.

You may wish to modify items such as the default directory for user documents.

The Save Tab

12.   Make sure the Save tab is active.

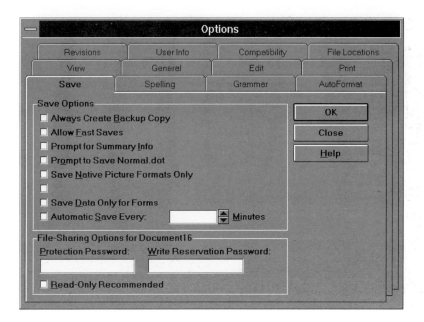

From here you can activate options such as automatic document save.

A "Fast save" records only the changes to a document (in addition to the original information) at time of saving. This is quicker, but will make less efficient use of disk space.

The sharing options allow you to protect your document with a password. "Write reservation" will prompt the user for the password when they attempt to save their changes.

The Spelling Tab

13.   Make sure the Spelling tab is active.

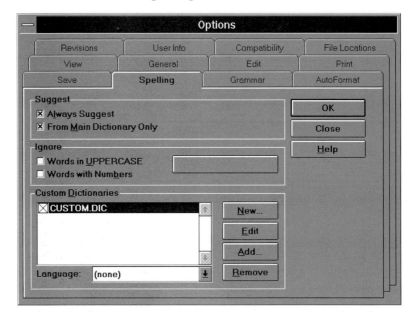

From here you can choose your Spell Checking preferences, and set up new Custom Dictionaries.

A Custom Dictionary could be used to store technical jargon, for example. If you were checking a technical document, you would activate the appropriate Custom dictionary by clicking on the checkbox in the custom dictionaries list.

To set up a new custom dictionary:

1.   Click on "New", then enter a filename ending with the ".DIC" extension code and press Return.

When Spell checking you can choose to add words to any of the custom dictionaries. You can also make changes to the dictionary file directly from the Options dialog box:

2.   Use the "Edit" button to view the dictionary as a Word document.

The Grammar Tab

14.   Click on the Grammar tab.

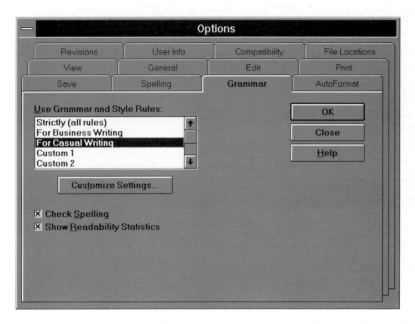

Use this dialog to set your Grammar checking preferences.

These options are covered in Chapter 8 "Automatic Features".

The AutoFormat Tab

15. Make sure the AutoFormat tab is active.

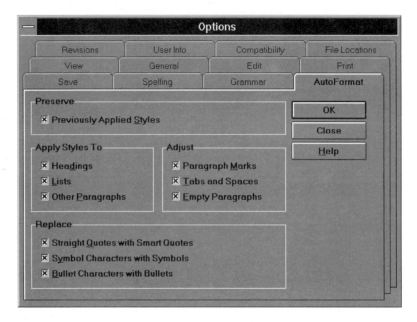

Use this dialog to choose the extent to which AutoFormat will change your document.

Note that you can also access this dialog directly from the AutoFormat dialog box.

See Chapter 9 "Styles" for a description of the AutoFormat process.

CHAPTER

14

Sections

THIS CHAPTER COVERS

in easy steps

Columns

1.   Open a document.

2.   Switch to Page Layout View.

Text is initially set out in one column which stretches across most of the page (according to margins and indents).

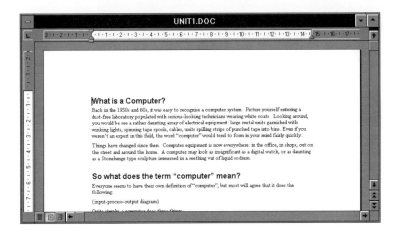

3.   Drag on the Columns icon downwards and to the right to define a three column layout:

The Columns icon

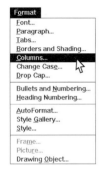

4.   Alternatively, choose "Columns" from the Format menu.

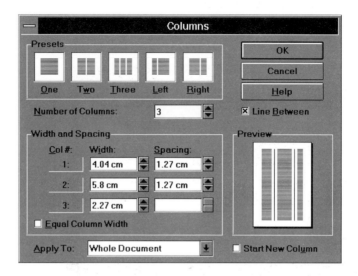

5.   Use the Width and Spacing options to change to three
      irregular columns with a vertical line in between, if
      required.

Your new column layout will apply to the entire document. To
use different layouts in the same document, it is necessary to
divide it into Sections.

Sections

1. Click an Insertion Point part of the way through your document (between paragraphs).

2. Choose "Break" from the Insert menu.

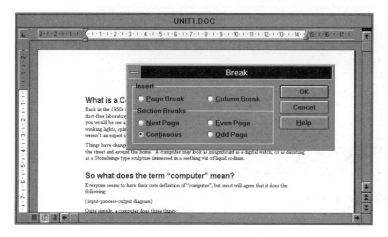

The Break dialog box appears.

3. Choose the "Continuous" option, under Section Breaks.

4. Click "OK".

In Normal view, you can see the section break as a horizontal dotted line:

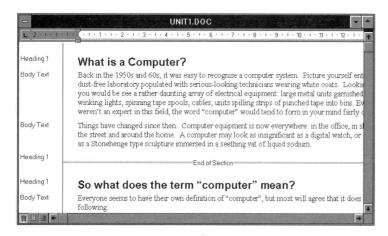

Our document is now divided into two sections.

Using Columns with Sections

1.   Make sure you are using a document which has been
     divided into two sections.

2.   Click an Insertion point somewhere in the second section,
     then choose "Columns" from the Format menu:

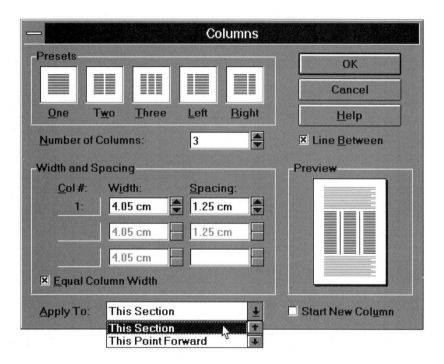

3.   Set the Number of Columns to 3.

4.   From the "Apply to" pop-up menu, make sure that the
     Columns are applied to "This Section" only.

5.   Click "OK".

You now have a mixed column layout:

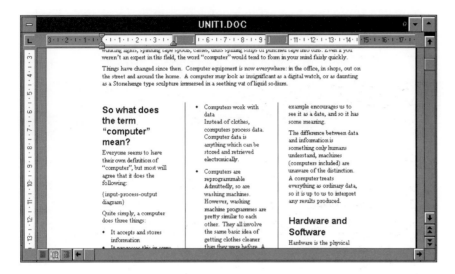

6. You can also adjust the width of columns by dragging the columns markers in the ruler:

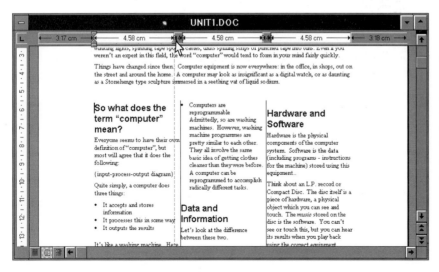

TIP

If you drag with the Alt key held down, Word will display the horizontal measurements in the ruler.

Column Breaks

You can force text to start in a new column by inserting a hard break.

7.   Place your Insertion Point and choose "Break" from the Insert menu.

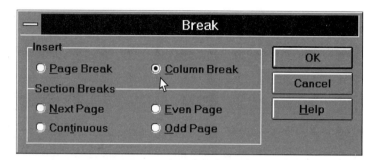

This will force the text after the Insertion Point into a new column.

Balancing Columns

8.   Click an Insertion Point about two thirds of the way down the last column and choose "Break" from the Insert menu.

9.   Insert a "Continuous" Section Break.

The columns are balanced to within one line of each other.

In this example there is also a Page Break after the three column section.

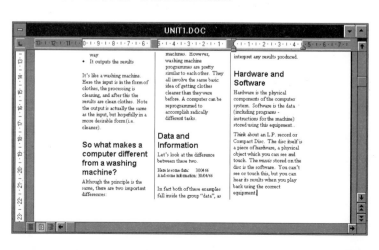

The Page Setup Dialog Box

The Layout Tab

1.   Place the Insertion Point anywhere within one section.

2.   Choose "Page Setup" from the File menu.

3.   Activate the Layout tab.

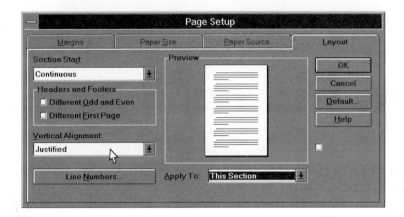

4.   Choose "Justified" from the Vertical Alignment pop-up menu.

This will add space between paragraphs so that the text stretches between the top and bottom margins.

5.   Make sure that the Apply To pop-up menu is set to "This Section".

6.   Click "OK".

Other Tabs

Note that the other Page Layout tabs can also be set to apply to sections rather than the whole document

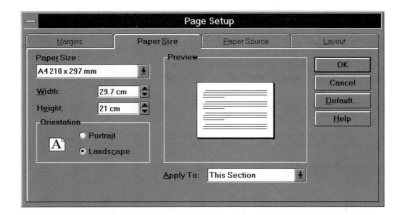

This means that you can set up a document using a variety of different margins, column layouts, paper sizes and orientations.

15

The Outline View

The Outliner

The Outliner allows you to work with your document as a structure of different levels of heading and body text.

Here is some text in Normal view...

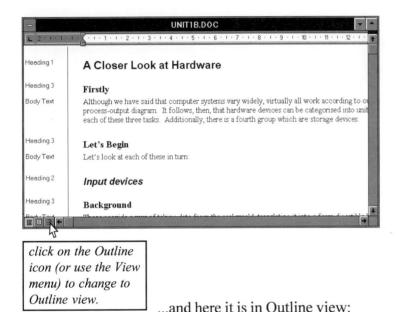

click on the Outline icon (or use the View menu) to change to Outline view.

...and here it is in Outline view:

The Outline Toolbar

You can use this to control your text structure:

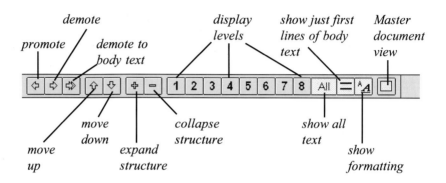

We'll examine these in turn.

Concepts

Your Styles list contains styles "Heading 1", "Heading 2", "Heading 3" and so on. Each of these is seen as being on a different level, ranging from 1 to 8.

For example, the style "Heading 1" is seen as the main heading of the document. For every instance of "Heading 1", the text may be broken down into several instances of "Heading 2". These in turn may break down on another level to "Heading 3", and so on.

If you have a large document, with a great deal of text and a complex heading system, the Outliner can provide you with a shorthand way of viewing and manipulating this structure.

The Promote Icon

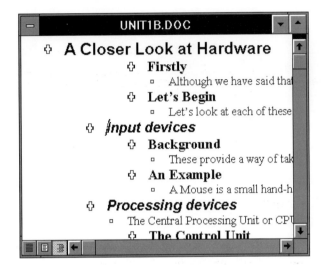

Click inside a line of text, then on the Promote icon.

If possible, the line is promoted to the higher Heading level:

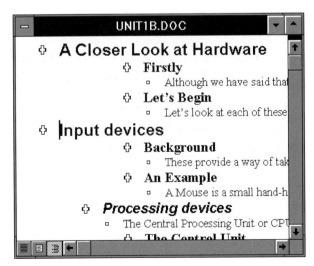

The demote button does the reverse.

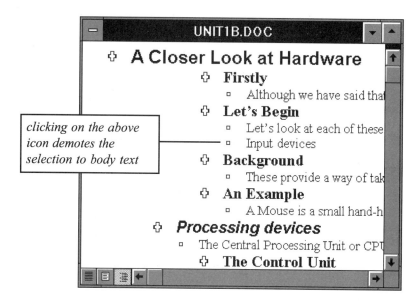

Demote to Body Text

clicking on the above icon demotes the selection to body text

Collapse &

Expand

Collapsed text only displays the higher levels. Each time you click on the collapse button the selection removes a level of detail. Expand reverses this.

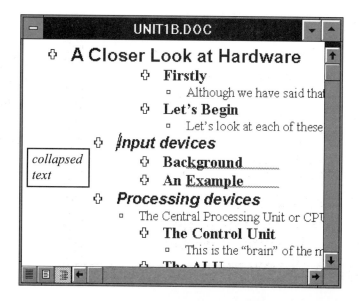

collapsed text

HINT

You can also collapse and expand by double-clicking on the + or - icon in the margin next to the outline text itself.

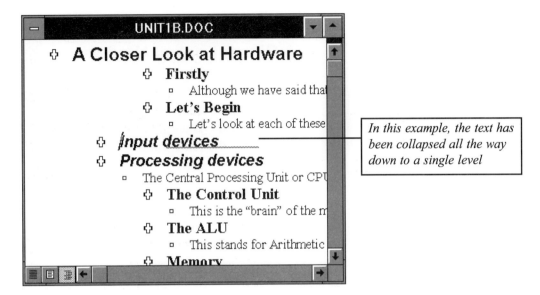

In this example, the text has been collapsed all the way down to a single level

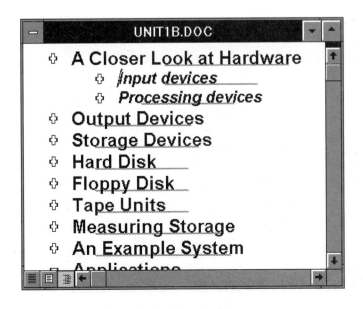

The Level Icons

Click on any of these to display only headings of that level and above:

2

In this example, only level 2 and above is on display.

This example shows
everything on level 3
and above:

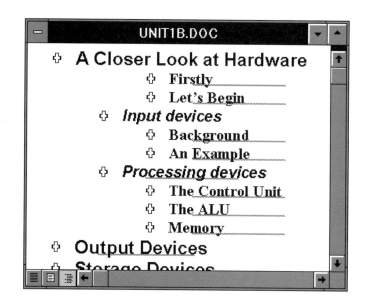

View All

This icon displays everything including all headings and body
text.

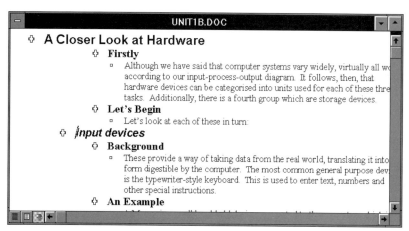

View First Lines Only

This button shows only the first line of each paragraph of body text.

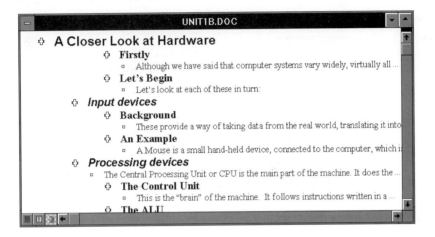

Selecting and Dragging

You can move lines simply by selecting, then dragging to a new position:

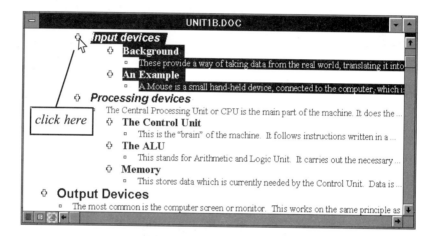

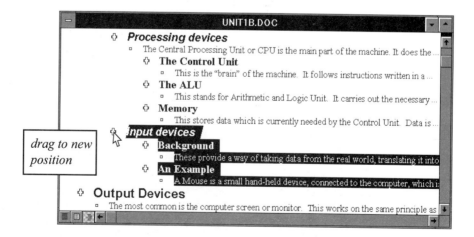

16

Tables

in easy steps

Tables

A Table is a way of organising text into rows and columns.

To Add a Table

1. Place the Insertion Point on a blank line in the document.

2. Click and drag downwards and to the right on the Table icon in the Toolbar.

the Table icon

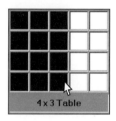

The further you drag, the larger the table. In this case we're creating a table of 4 rows and 3 columns.

The table is inserted into your document:

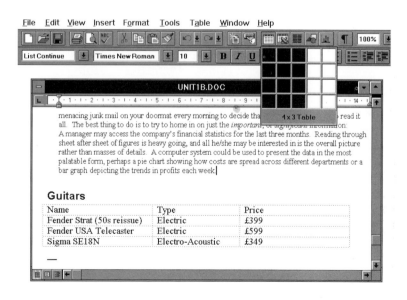

An example table

Resizing Rows & Columns

You can resize a column by moving your Mouse pointer to the border between the columns: it will turn into a black double headed arrow ◄┃► .

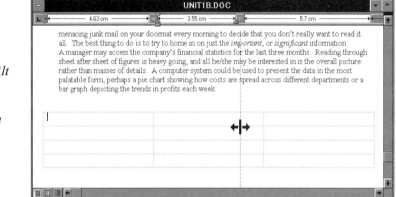

Hold down the Alt key to see the column measurements in the ruler.

You can resize rows in the same way.

Entering Text

You can add text to your table by clicking in each cell in turn. All the normal formatting commands still apply.

A quick way to get to the next cell is to press the Tab key. Shift + Tab takes you back to the previous cell.

TIP

If you actually need to enter a Tab character, press Control + Tab.

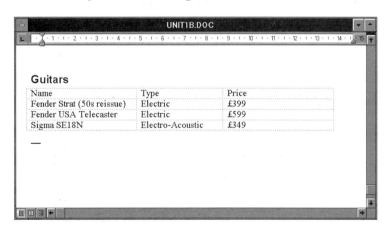

NOTE

*You can have more than one line within each cell. The Table row will
expand automatically to accommodate any extra text:*

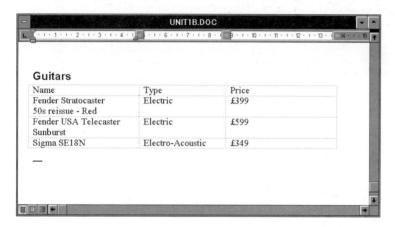

Formatting

You can format a whole row or column at once. To select a row
drag across or click in the space just to its left.

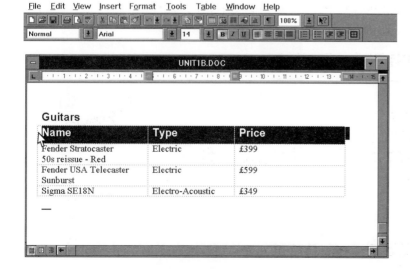

*The same applies
to columns. To
select click
slightly above the
top cell of the
column.*

Inserting a Row or Column

1. Select the column to the right of where you'd like the new cells (keep the mouse pointer in the column).

2. Holding down the right Mouse button, choose "Insert Columns" from the pop-up menu.

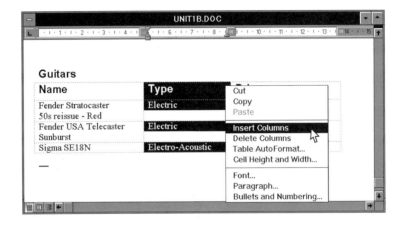

The new column appears:

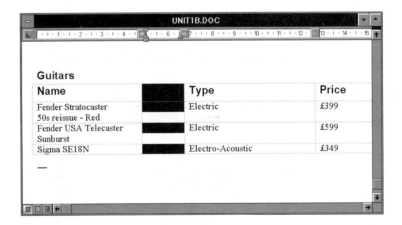

Similarly, to insert rows, select the row above which you want to insert a row. Holding down the right Mouse button, choose "Insert Rows" from the pop-up menu.

Cutting & Pasting

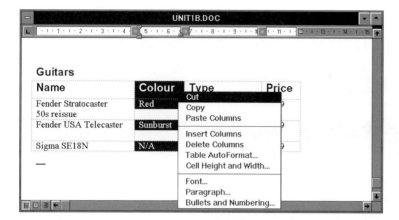

Select the row/ column or cells.

Holding down the right Mouse button, choose "Cut" from the pop-up menu.

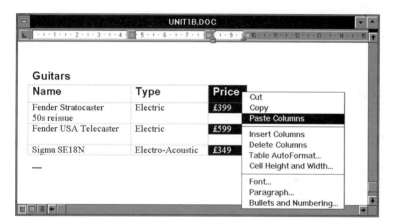

Select the destination row/column or cells.

Hold down the right Mouse button to access the "Paste" option.

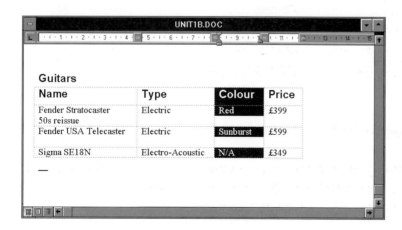

The text is pasted back into the table.

Selecting the Entire Table

Choose "Select Table" from the Table menu, or type Alt +
Numeric keypad "5" (with Num Lock Off).

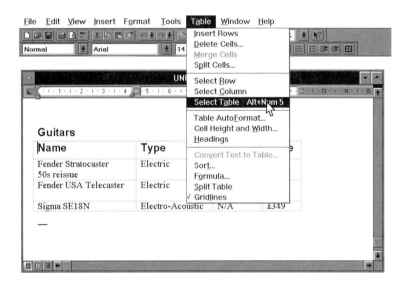

Controlling Height & Width

1. Select the cell(s) to change.

2. Choose "Cell Height and Width" from the Table menu.

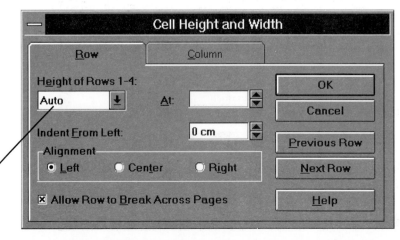

"Auto" sizes
rows/columns
according to
the text inside.

3. Click on the Row tab, then the Column tab to see all the options available.

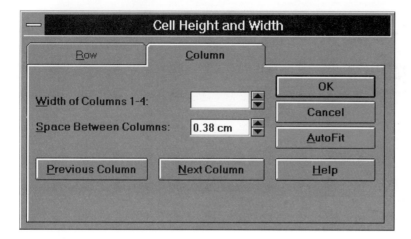

The AutoFit button proportions the column widths on the basis of the table size and the contents of the columns.

Merging Cells

1. Select the adjacent cells to be merged.

2. Choose "Merge Cells" from the Table menu.

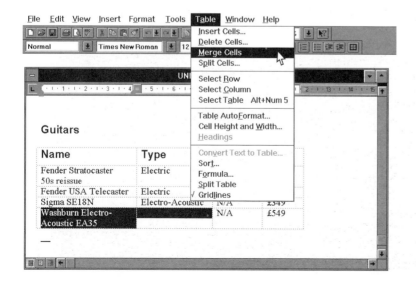

The cells have now been merged into one:

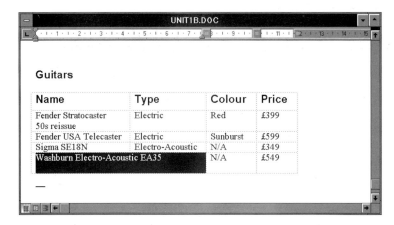

Formulae

In this example we have a column of figures to be added up.

1.   Click in the cell which is the destination for the calculation.

2.   Choose "Formula" from the Edit menu.

3.   Enter the formula or select from the list of "Paste functions".

4.   Choose the Number format and click "OK".

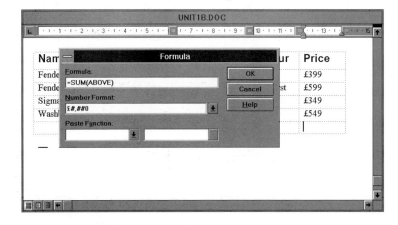

The result is added as a field, which will be recalculated if the numbers above change:

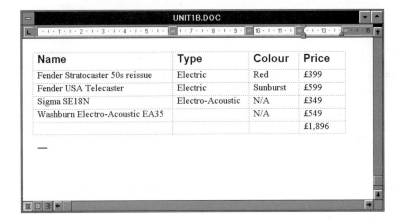

The example below uses the AVERAGE function:

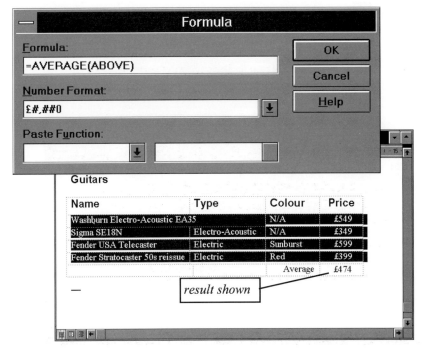

result shown

The number format in this case instructs Word to display a pound sign followed by the digits (which will contain commas to separate thousands).

Whole numbers with no decimal point will be shown.

Note the "0" means that there must always be at least one digit displayed (even if it's zero).

Sorting

1.   Select the Table

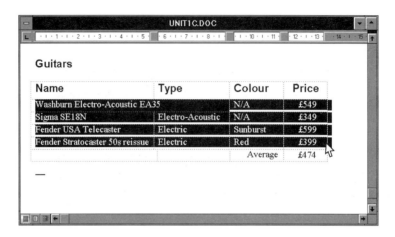

2.   Choose "Sort" from the Table menu:

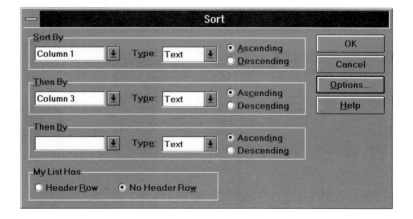

3.   Set the Sort options.

In this case we're sorting alphabetically on the basis of the text in Column 1. Any cells in Column 1 containing the same text will be sorted on the basis of Column 3.

4.   Click "OK".

The rows of the table are moved around so that the text in Column 1 reads alphabetically.

| UNIT1C.DOC |

Guitars

Name	Type	Colour	Price
Fender Stratocaster 50s reissue	Electric	Red	£399
Fender USA Telecaster	Electric	Sunburst	£599
Sigma SE18N	Electro-Acoustic	N/A	£349
Washburn Electro-Acoustic EA35		N/A	£549
		This Month's Average Price	£474

NOTE

Sorting is very useful when using your table as a database, and is accessible as an icon from the Database toolbar. Look at Chapter 17, "Mail Merging" for more details about this.

Borders and Shading

1. Select either the entire table or just a range of cells.

2. Choose "Borders and Shading" from the Format menu.

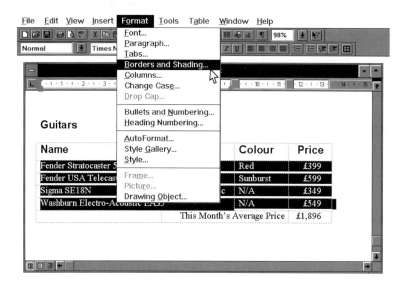

3. If necessary activate the Borders tab, and choose your
    borders options.

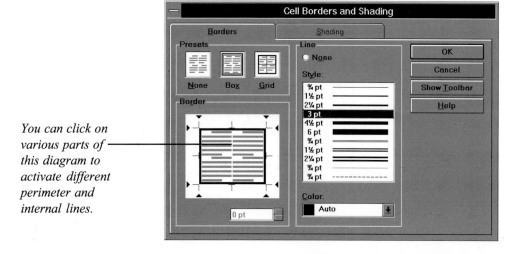

*You can click on
various parts of
this diagram to
activate different
perimeter and
internal lines.*

4. Now click on the Shading tab and set your shading (fill) preferences.

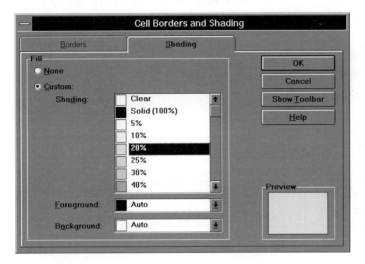

5. Click "OK".

Your selected cells now have a border and shade applied:

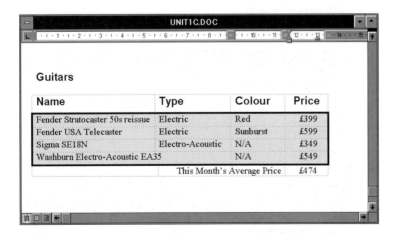

Internal border lines

In this example we've used the Borders dialog box to set up a style for the lines *inside* the selected area:

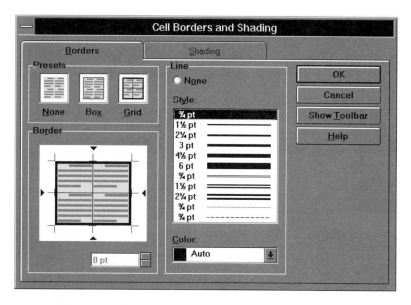

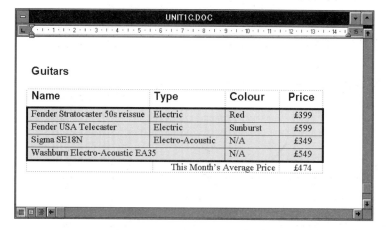

The Borders Toolbar

You can activate the Borders toolbar either from the View menu
("Toolbars" command) or by holding down the right Mouse
button on one of the existing toolbars.

Using the Toolbar

1. Select the cell(s) to be formatted.

2. Select a line style then click on the appropriate line icon:

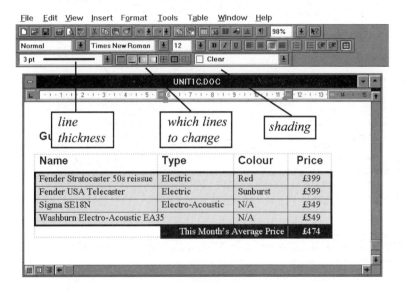

In this case
we're about to
apply a 3 point
line style to the
bottom, left and
right borders of
the selected cell
area.

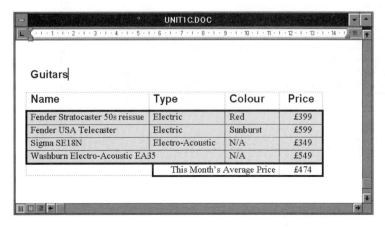

Changing Shading

1.   Select the cell(s) to change.

2.   Choose a fill option from the pop-up menu in the toolbar.

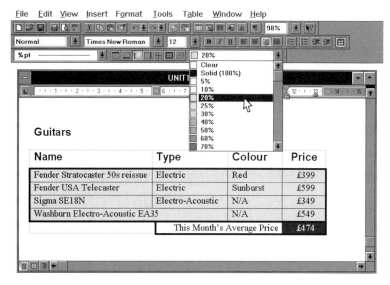

Using Borders on Ordinary Text

Note you can set borders and shading on any paragraph:

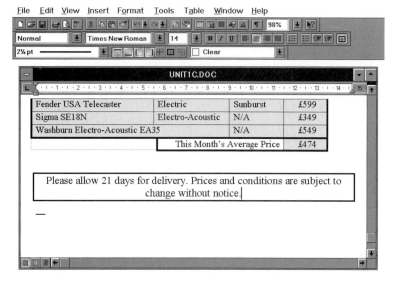

1.   Select a normal paragraph of text.

2.   Choose "Borders and Shading" from the Format menu.

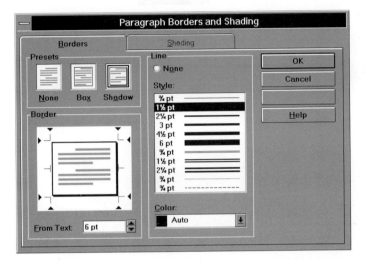

Notice that the options in this dialog box are slightly different depending upon whether the selection is a table or ordinary text.

Please allow 21 days for delivery. Prices and conditions are subject to change without notice.

Converting Tabulated Text into a Table

1.   Select the tabulated text

For more information on tabulation see Chapter 12 "Rulers and Tabulation".

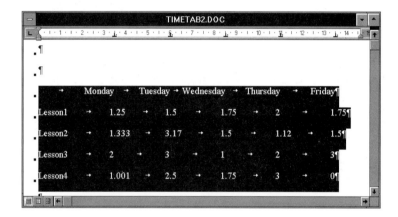

2.   Choose "Convert Text to Table" from the Table menu.

If you clicked "OK" at this point, the table would be set up with the correct number of rows and columns, but would still require manual formatting.

3.   Click on the "AutoFormat" button.

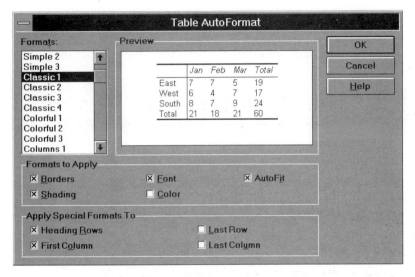

4.   Choose a table style from the "Formats" list, referring to the Preview box for guidance.

5.   Select which aspects of formatting are to be applied.

6.   Click "OK".

NOTE

You can reverse this process with the "Convert Table to Text" command from the Table menu.

Gridlines

These show you how your table is divided into cells. Sometimes it is useful to switch them off to get a better idea of how the table will look when printed.

You can do this by selecting "Gridlines" from the Table menu:

	Monday	Tuesday	Wednesday	Thursday	Friday
Lesson1	1.25	1.5	1.75	2	1.75
Lesson2	1.333	3.17	1.5	1.12	1.5
Lesson3	2	3	1	2	3
Lesson4	1.001	2.5	1.75	3	0

TIMETAB2.DOC

Table AutoFormat

Note that you can apply AutoFormat to an existing table.

1.   Select the table, or click an Insertion Point.

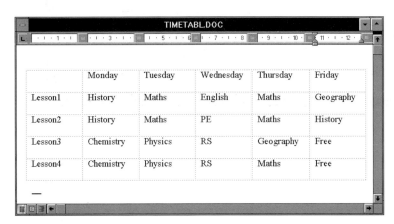

TIMETABL.DOC

	Monday	Tuesday	Wednesday	Thursday	Friday
Lesson1	History	Maths	English	Maths	Geography
Lesson2	History	Maths	PE	Maths	History
Lesson3	Chemistry	Physics	RS	Geography	Free
Lesson4	Chemistry	Physics	RS	Maths	Free

2.   Choose "Table AutoFormat" from the Table menu.

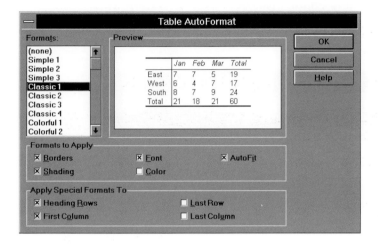

3.   Select the required options.

4.   Click "OK".

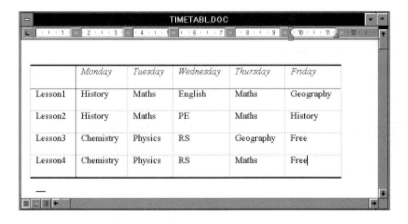

The Table Wizard

Like the Wizard Templates, this feature automatically creates a formatted table on the basis of a series of questions.

1.   Choose "Insert Table" from the Table menu.

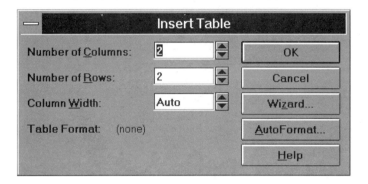

2.   Click on the "Wizard" button.

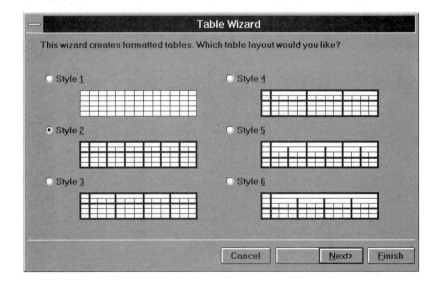

3.   Choose the Table layout and click on "Next".

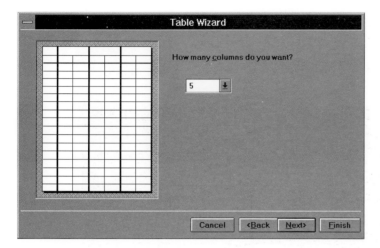

4.   Enter the number of columns and click "Next".

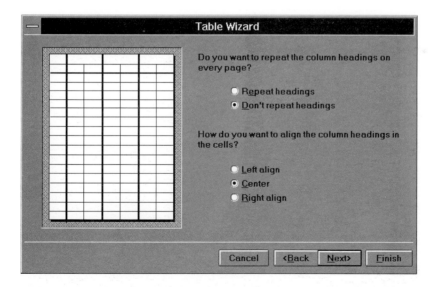

5.   Select the column headings options and click "Next".

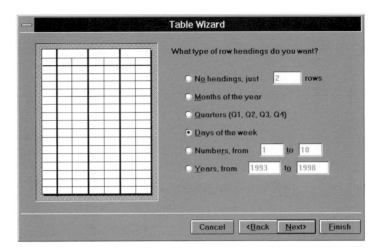

6.   Select the row heading type and click "Next".

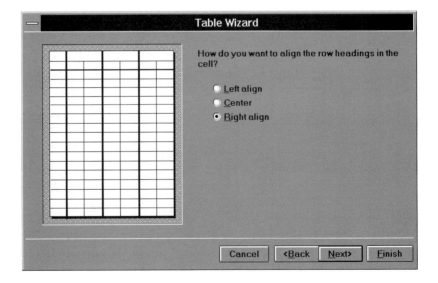

7.   Select the row alignment option and click "Next".

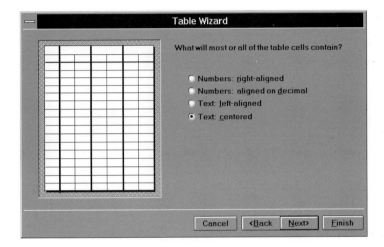

8. Enter the default cell option and click "Next".

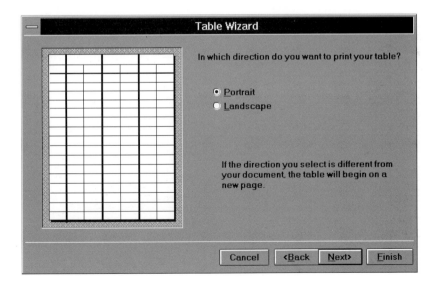

9. Choose "Portrait" or "Landscape" orientation and click "Next".

10. Finally, click
on "Finish" to
generate the
table...

The new formatted table is created.

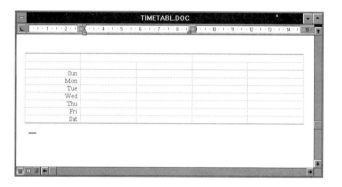

You can now add and edit your table items.

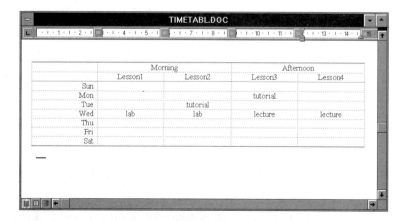

17

Mail Merging

in easy steps

Concepts

Mail Merging involves the merging of two files, a text document and a datafile.

An example

Let's say you wanted to send a standard business letter to 100 of your clients. Your text document would be the letter itself, specially marked with fields reserved for the name, address and other details needed to personalise it for a particular customer.

Your datafile would be a database containing the 100 customer records. Each customer record would consist of fields which contain the information needed to personalise the business letter.

The Data Source

A row of the table can be thought of as a data record.

The columns divide these into a number of fields, each of which has a name in the top line of the table.

This can simply be a table set up within a normal Word document. Word can view any regular table as a database.

See Chapter 16 "Tables" for more information about Table features.

1.   Switch on the Database toolbar by choosing "Toolbars"
      from the View menu, or by holding down the right Mouse
      button over an existing toolbar and selecting "Database"
      from the pop-up menu.

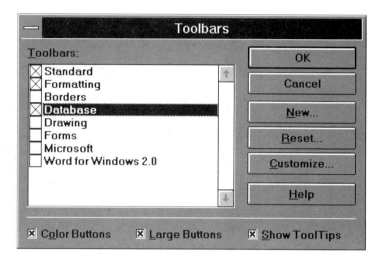

The Database Toolbar

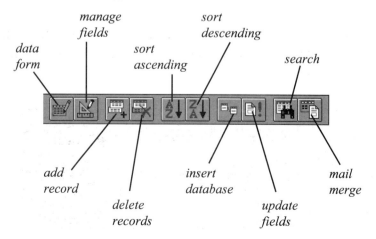

Sorting Data

1. Select the Column containing the data to be used as the basis for the sort.

2. Click on the Sort Ascending icon to sort the records (rows of tables) into alphabetic order.

NOTE

You can also use the Insert Database Icon to import data from another program such as Microsoft Access.

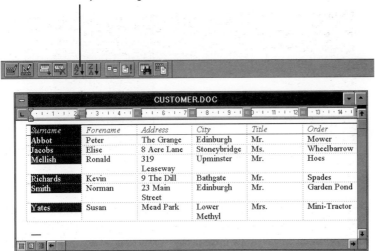

Manage Fields

Click on the Manage fields icon to add, remove or rename fields (column headings) using a dialog box rather than by operating on the table itself.

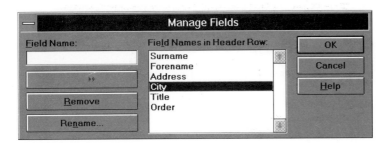

The Data Form

Use this icon to work with your data one record at a time via the
Data Form dialog box:

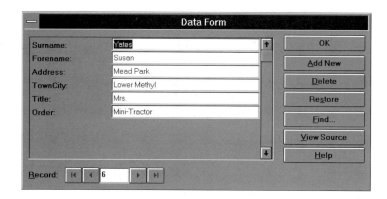

Find In Field

Click on this icon to access the Find in Field dialog box. From
here you can locate a record on the basis of the contents of any
field:

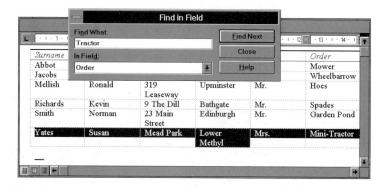

The Mail Merge Process

For this example, let's assume we've already saved our data source document on disk.

1. Choose "Mail Merge" from the Tools menu.

The Mail Merge Helper dialog box appears.

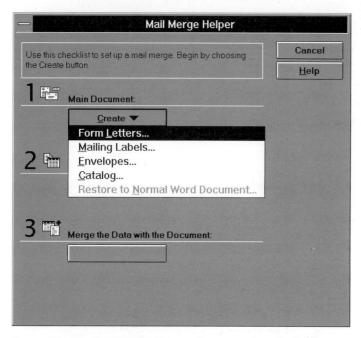

2. Under "Main Document", open the Create pop-up menu and choose "Form Letters".

3. Choose "New Main Document".

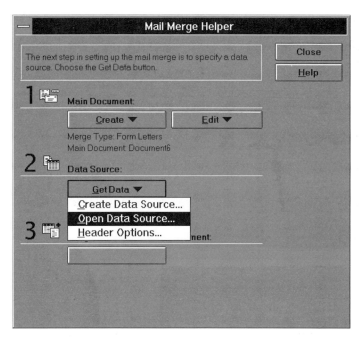

4. Select "Open Data Source" from the Get Data pop-up menu.

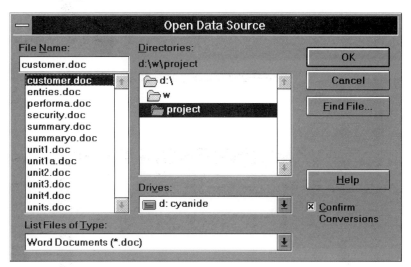

5. Locate the data source document and click "OK".

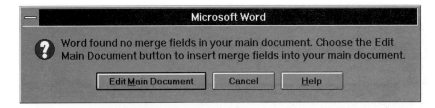

6.   Click on "Edit Main Document".

The Mail Merge toolbar will also appear.

7.   Enter the text for your main document. To insert a merge
      field open the Insert Merge Field pop-up menu and choose
      the required field:

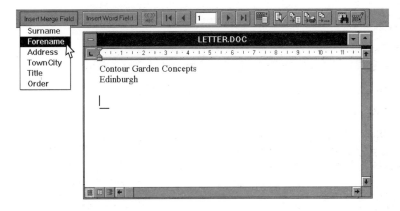

The field is added:

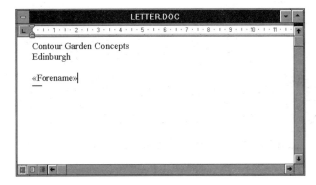

8.   Complete the main document inserting Merge Fields where necessary.

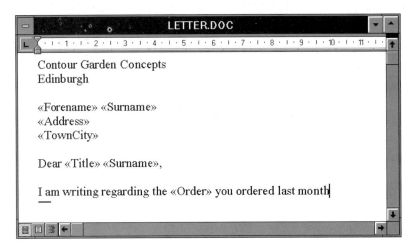

9.   Use the preview button to see how your document will look using actual details from the data source.

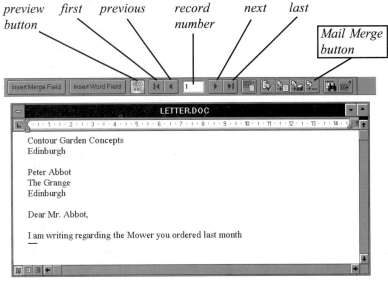

10.   When you're ready, click the "Mail Merge" button.

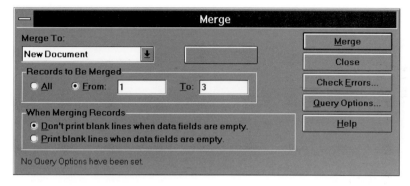

11.   Select the Merge options, and click "Merge".

The data will be merged with the main document to produce all the copies required.

Other Options

1.   From the Merge dialog, click on "Query Options".

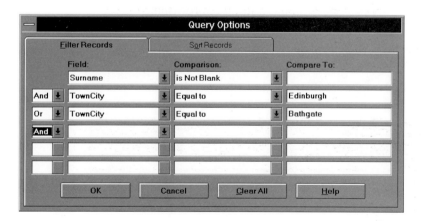

2.   If necessary, activate the Filter Records tab.

From here you can instruct Word to use only some of the data records, according to various comparisons accessed from the pop-up lists.

3.   Click on the Sort tab.

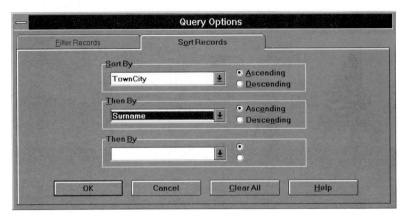

You can use this dialog to specify the order in which the merged
letters will be created.

4.   Finally, click "OK" to return to the Mail Merge Helper.

5.   Click "Merge" and continue as normal.

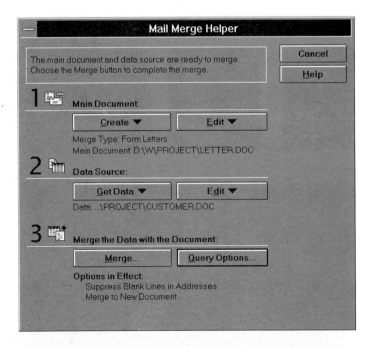

CHAPTER

18

Forms

Forms

We have already seen how to use a form in Chapter 10 "Templates". In this chapter we'll set up our own form from scratch.

The Forms Toolbar

1. Switch on the Forms toolbar by holding down the right Mouse button from within an existing toolbar, and selecting Forms from the pop-up menu.

2. To insert a form text field (the variable text in a form), click the Insertion Point at the appropriate place, then click on the Text field button.

text field

▷

The text field is added:

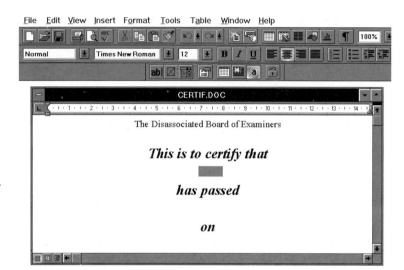

HINT

To see fields as grey bars make sure field shading is selected from the Options dialog box (View tab).

3.   Double-click on the field to access its options.

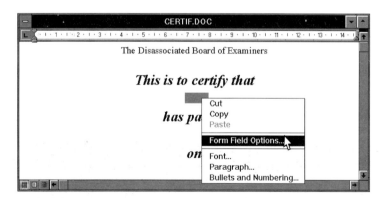

You can also access the options by holding down on the field with the right Mouse button:

The Form Field dialog appears:

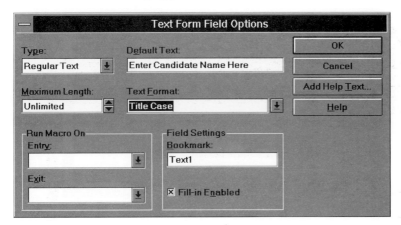

4. From here you can set options such as the default contents and the maximum length of the field. Click "OK" when you've finished.

Drop-Down Lists

5. Click on this icon to create a drop-down list of choices to select from.

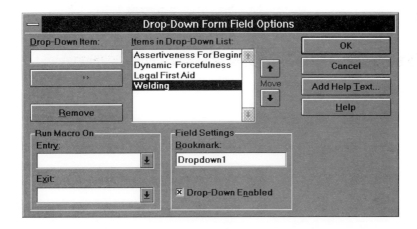

6.   Enter the list of options and click "OK".

Other Types of Form Fields

This example sets up a text field to display the date in longhand form.

Checkboxes

Click on this symbol to create a checkbox field.

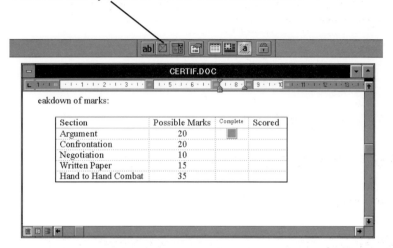

A checkbox is a simple on/off switch activated with the Spacebar and used for a Yes/No answer.

Double-click on the field to see the checkbox options:

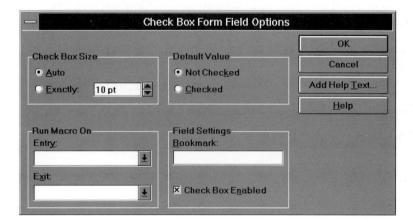

Number boxes

To create a number box to enter numeric data:

1.   Create a text field.

2.   Double-click to access the options dialog.

3.   Select "Number" from the Type pop-up menu.

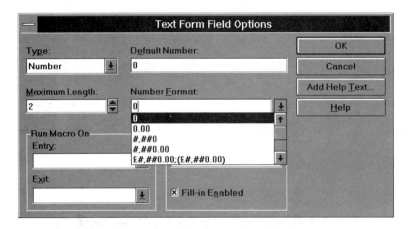

Finishing the Preparation

1.   Choose "Protect Document" from the Tools menu.

This will prevent you from accidently changing the form but allow you to 'fill-in' the form.

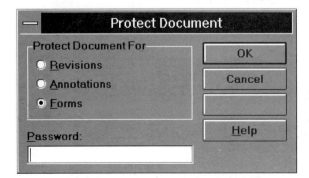

2.   Select "Forms" and click "OK".

The preparation of the form is now complete.

Using the Form

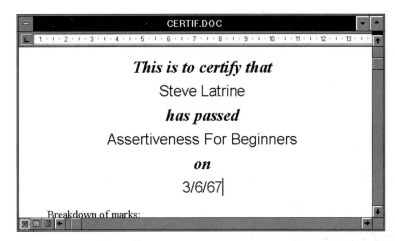

Using the form is a simple process, since only the field value can be changed. To move to the next field press Tab, or Shift + Tab to go back.

In the example above, the date is being entered.

As soon as the Return key is pressed, the date's formatting changes to that specified in the field options dialog.

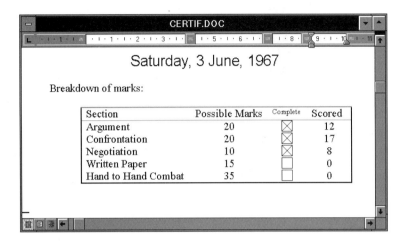

The form can be filled in by someone much less skilled in the operation of Word. All they need to know is how to move between fields and type/edit text.

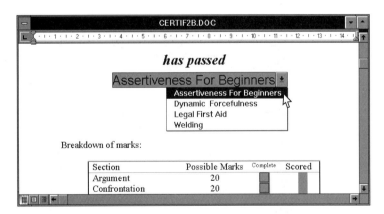

The drop-down list box is particularly useful if the same text is required again and again.

CHAPTER

19

Graphical
Features

Using Clipart

Word has its own directory of Clipart illustrations.

1.   Click an Insertion Point at the destination for the graphic.

2.   Choose "Picture" from the Insert menu.

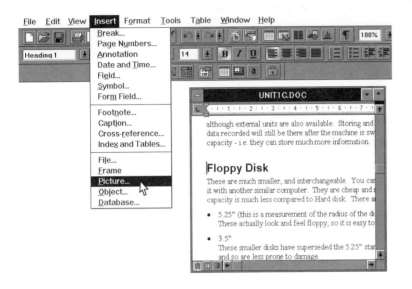

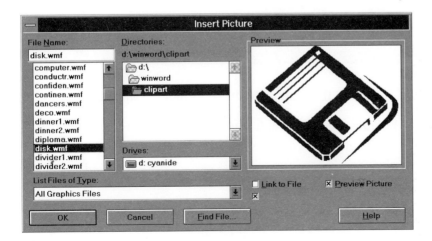

3.   Locate the file you require and click "OK".

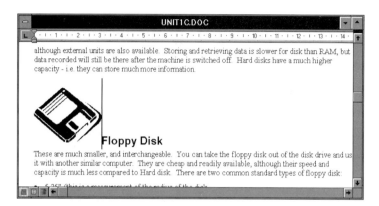

The Picture is inserted as if it was a large character.

Manipulating Graphics

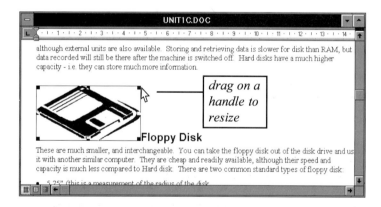

drag on a handle to resize

1.   Click on the graphic to make its handles appear.

The handles are eight small square blocks which allow you to change the graphic's dimensions.

2.   Drag on a handle to resize the picture.

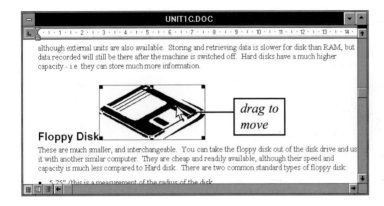

3.   Drag anywhere within the object to move it to a new position.

Note that the graphic is treated like a text item, so when you drag it to a new position, the surrounding text moves to make room.

Framed Graphics

1.   Select the picture.

2.   Click on the Insert Frame icon in the Forms toolbar, or choose "Frame" from the Insert menu.

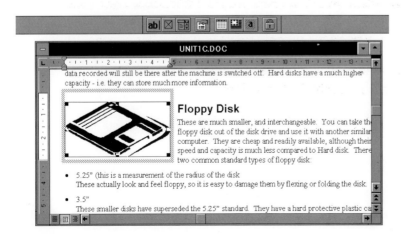

The graphic now inhabits a Frame, and is no longer part of the text.

The text flows around the Frame.

The Format Picture Dialog

1.   Select the Picture.

2.   Choose "Picture" from the Format menu.

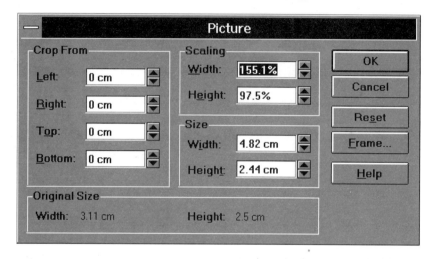

From here you can numerically alter the scale, size and crop parameters of the picture.

The Format Frame Dialog

1.   Select the Frame and choose "Frame" from the Format menu to change the frame options.

You can adjust the text wrap, and the frame's position in relation to the neighbouring paragraph.

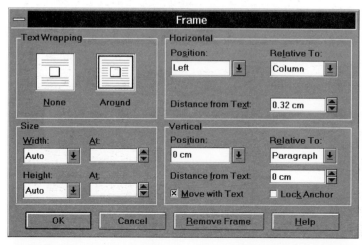

Cropping a Picture

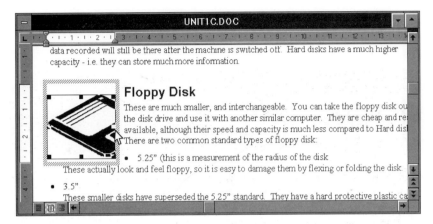

To crop (i.e. cut away part of a picture), simply drag inwards on one of its handles while holding down the Shift key.

NOTE

Cropping is non-destructive. This means that you can restore the rest of the picture by Shift-dragging outwards on a handle.

Frame Borders and Shading

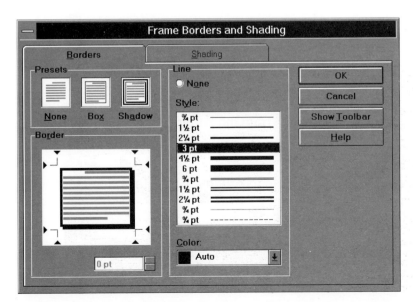

Select the frame and choose "Borders and Shading" from the Format menu.

Note you can also use the Borders toolbar.

The above example illustrates the shadow border effect.

Reset Picture

1.   Select the Picture.

2.   Choose "Picture" from the Format menu.

3.   Click "Reset", then "OK".

The Picture is restored to its original size with nothing cropped out.

Inserting a Blank Frame

1. With nothing selected, click on the Insert frame icon.

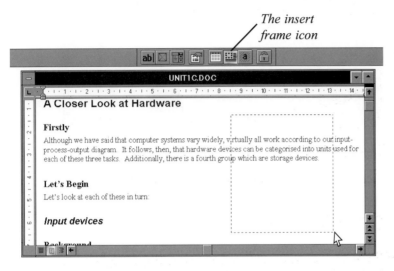

The insert frame icon

2. Click and drag over the frame area.

A new blank frame is created. You can fill this with text or graphics. Simply click inside to enter and format text as normal.

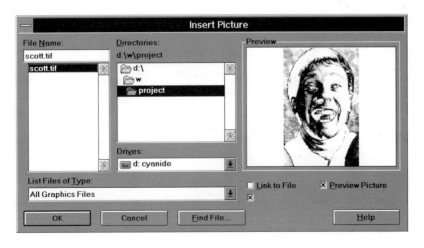

3. To insert an image select the blank frame, choose "Picture" from the Insert menu and locate the desired file.

HINT

To prevent your document becoming too large, click on the "Link to File" option.

This means Word will not include the graphic data as part of the document, but instead access the original file, when necessary.

▷

The picture appears in the frame:

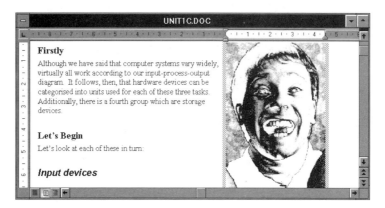

Types of Graphic File

Word can import many different types of graphic file format.
WMF, CGM, WPG, DRW, EPS and PCT files normally contain
draw-type objects which can be scaled up or down with no loss
in quality (because they are stored as mathematical objects).

On the other hand BMP, PCX, TIF and GIF files are bitmapped:
the image is stored as a structure of tiny dots/blocks. Be careful
not to enlarge these pictures too much, or the dots will become
very noticeable, causing a marked deterioration in quality.

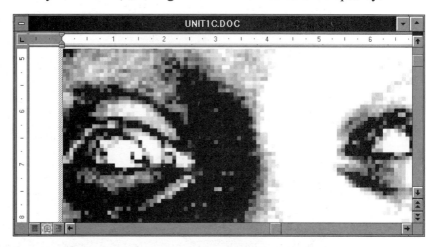

CHAPTER

20

Charts

THIS CHAPTER COVERS

in easy steps

Creating a New Chart

Charts provide a pictorial way of presenting numeric data. In Word this data is often entered into a table in the main part of the document.

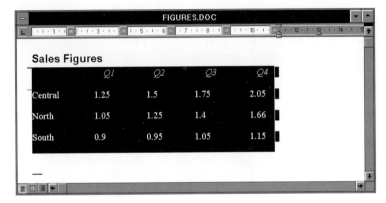

1.   Select the data in the table.

2.   Click on the Chart icon in the toolbar.

the chart icon

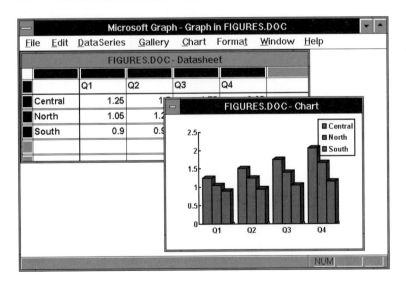

Microsoft Graph uses two main windows, one for the data and one for the chart itself.

The Microsoft Graph application opens, with the table data loaded automatically to generate a default-style chart.

Formatting the Chart

1.   Select an option from the Gallery menu. In this example we'll view our data as a 3-D Column chart:

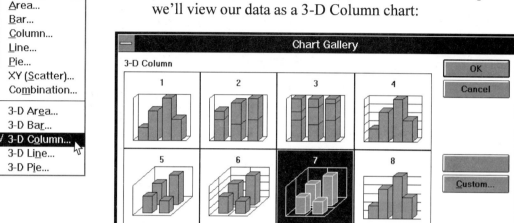

2.   Select the option you require and click "OK".

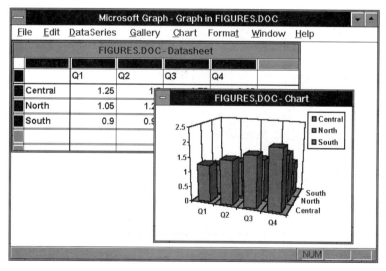

The chart is reformatted accordingly. Sometimes it is necessary to do a little more work to display the data effectively.

3.   Choose "3D-View" from the Format menu.

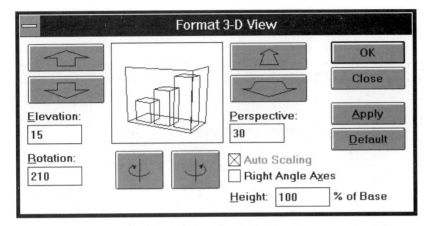

The original chart angle was 30 degrees.

4. Enter the 3-D options and click "OK".

In this example we have changed the angle of rotation to 210 degrees, so it has completely turned around:

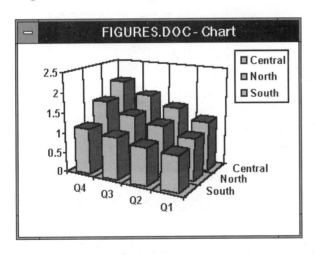

Further Enhancements

1.   Choose "Add Arrow" from the Chart menu.

An arrow appears.

2.   To position the arrow, drag on each end in turn.

3.   Use the "Patterns" command from the Format menu to customise the arrow attributes.

4.   Choose "Titles" from the Chart menu to add a chart title.

5.   Format the title using the "Font" command (Format menu).

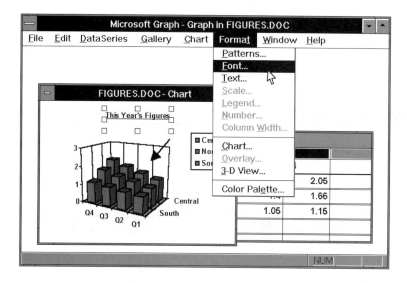

Area Patterns

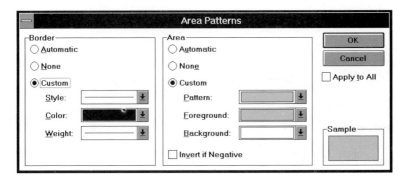

Double click on one of the bars on the chart to access the Area Patterns dialog box.

Importing Data

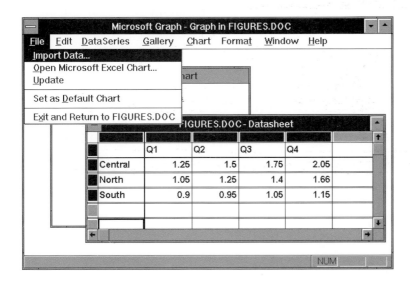

To bring in numeric data from an external source first click on the Datasheet window, then choose the "Import data" command from the File menu.

Number Format

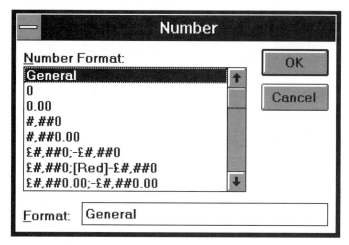

To access the number formatting options:

1.   Select some or all the cells in the Datasheet window.

2.   Choose "Number" from the Format menu.

Returning to Word

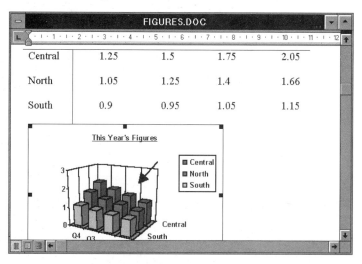

TIP

When you have a chart selected in Word, you can access Microsoft Graph at any time simply by double-clicking.

Close down Microsoft Graph by choosing "Exit" from the File menu. Click "Yes" when asked to update the graph in the document. The graph will appear at the current Insertion Point.

CHAPTER

21

The Drawing Tools

In easy Steps

Starting to Draw

To use Word's drawing facilities, click on the Drawing icon in the toolbar.

The drawing toolbar appears at the bottom of the screen. You can now draw on your page, either in a blank area or directly over the text.

NOTE

You can also access this from the "Toolbars" option in the view menu, or by holding down the right Mouse button on an existing toolbar.

The Drawing Toolbar

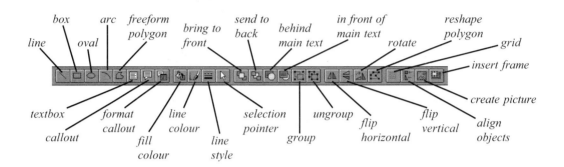

Creating Shapes

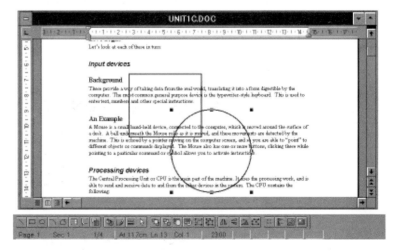

1. Select the appropriate shape tool.

2. Click and drag within the document to create the shape. For lines drag from one endpoint to the other, for boxes and ovals drag diagonally from one corner to the other.

3. Click on a shape with the Selection Pointer to select. Then you can drag it to another location, or resize by dragging directly on one of the shape's handles.

Lines and Fills

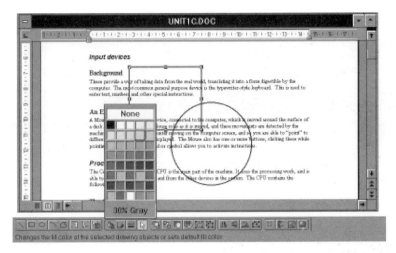

Click on a shape then use the fill and line icons to select colour, shading and line thickness.

Formatting Shapes

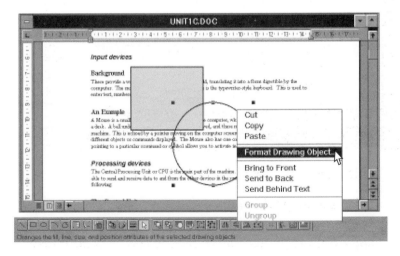

Select a shape then hold down the right Mouse button to access the "Format Drawing Object" command from the pop-up menu.

The Fill Tab

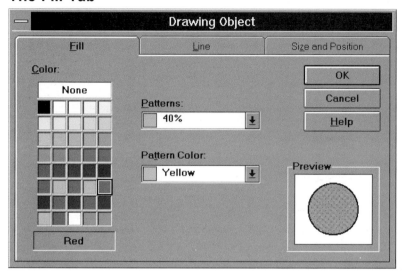

Set the object's fill attributes. Use the preview box for reference.

The Line Tab

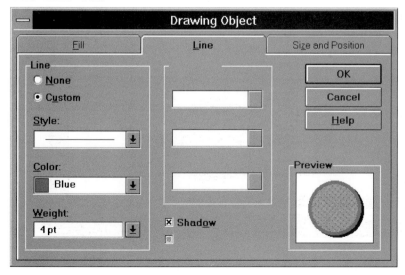

From here you can set the object's line options such as colour, thickness and shadow effect.

The Size and Position Tab

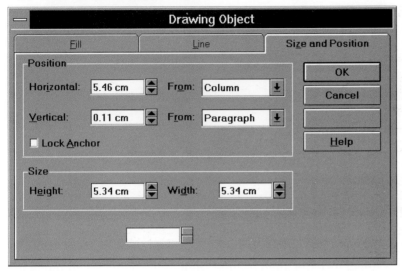

Here you can numerically control an object's size and position in
relation to the adjacent paragraph of text.

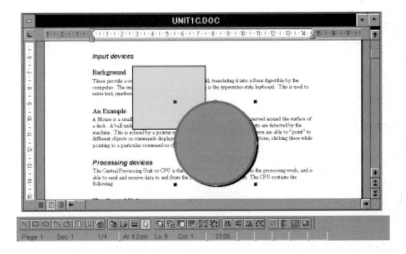

Front and Back

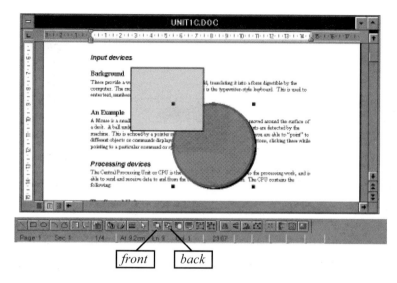

First select a shape, then use the front and back icons to move it
in front of or behind the other drawing shapes.

Selecting Multiple Objects

TIP

*You can also
select more than
one object at a
time by holding
down Shift as you
click.*

*Shift clicking a
second time will
deselect an object.*

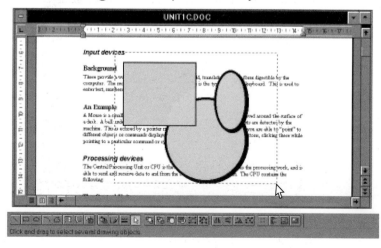

Click and drag with the pointer tool (starting in a blank space) to
create a selection box. When you release the Mouse button, all
objects completely ensnared will be selected.

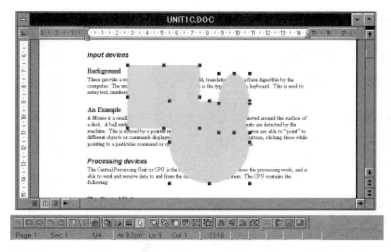

In this example we selected three objects then applied a line style of "none".

Send Behind Text Layer

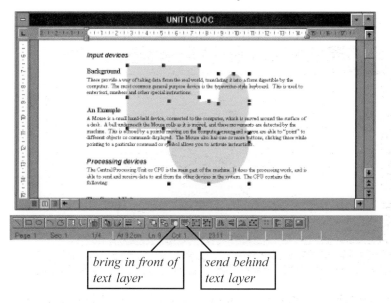

bring in front of
text layer

send behind
text layer

You can bring objects either in front of or send behind the main text in the document by clicking on these icons.

Aligning Objects

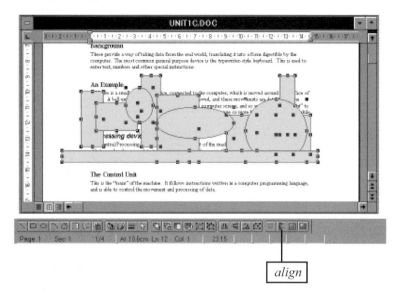

align

1. Select the objects to be aligned.

2. Click on the Align icon.

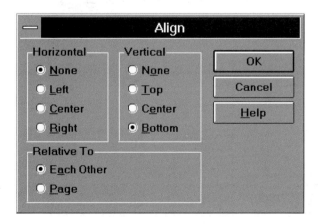

3. Select the Align options and click "OK".

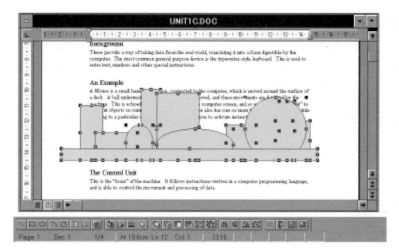

In this example we used "Vertical/Bottom" alignment to align these objects relative to each other.

Group/Ungroup

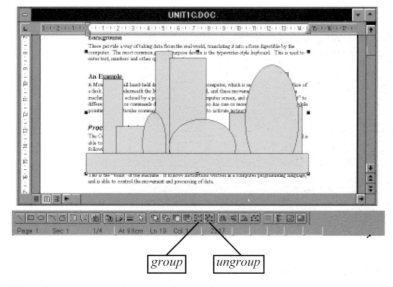

group *ungroup*

Once objects are combined into a group, they can be treated as a single element.

In this example we used the handles to stretch the entire shape.

Use the group tool to combine elements, ungroup reverses this process.

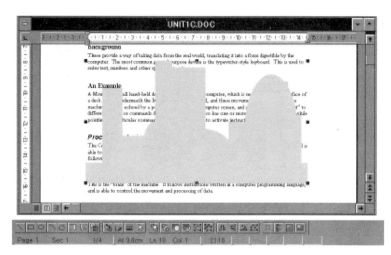

After stretching the grouped shape, we then used the line dialog box to set a line style of "none".

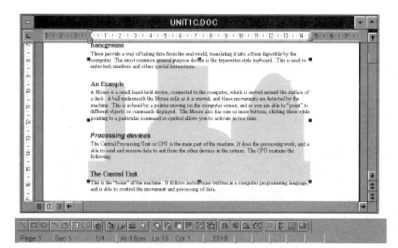

Finally, we sent the grouped object behind the text layer.

Cut, Copy and Paste

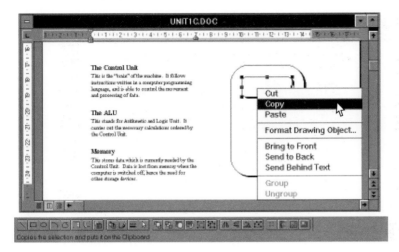

Keyboard shortcuts for Cut, Copy and Paste are Control + X, Control + C, and Control + V respectively.

If you chose Cut rather than Copy, the original shape would be removed.

1.   Select an object.

2.   Choose "Copy" from the right hand Mouse button pop-up menu.

3.   Choose "Paste" from the same menu.

Snap to Grid

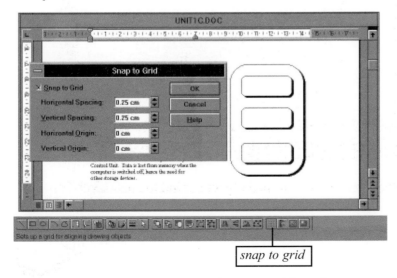

snap to grid

Use the snap to grid feature to help you position elements easily.

Callout Boxes

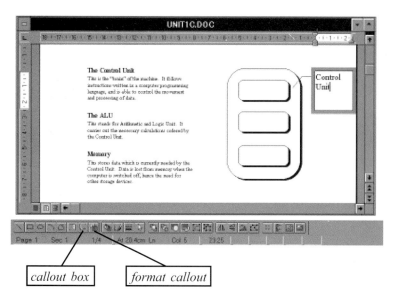

callout box   *format callout*

Callout boxes are useful ways of annotating a diagram. With the Callout box tool active, click/drag to create the line leading into the box. You can then move or resize the box, and enter its text.

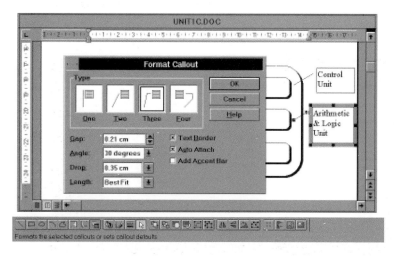

The Callout format icon lets you customise the Callout box options.

Freeform Polygons

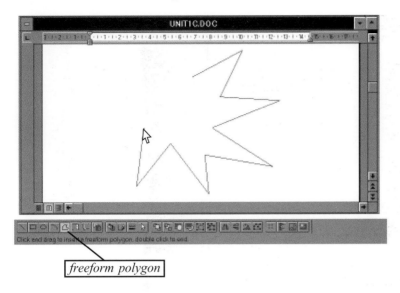

freeform polygon

1. Select the Freeform Polygon tool.

2. Click on each point in turn.

3. Click back on the start point to complete a closed shape. If you don't want it closed then double-click to end.

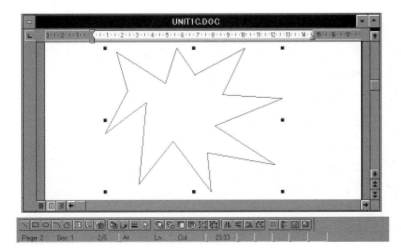

Reshaping a Polygon

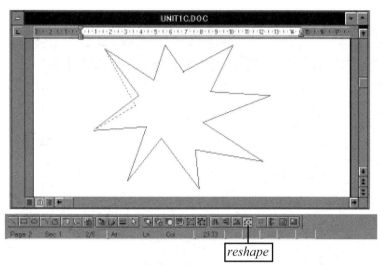

reshape

1.   Select the polygon and click on the reshape icon.

2.   Drag to move the corner points.

3.   Control-click on part of the line to create a new point.

4.   Control-click directly on a point to delete.

Create Picture

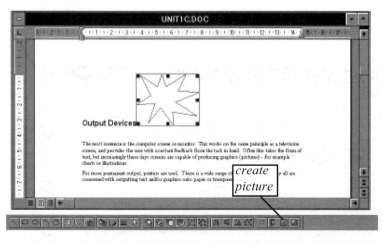

create picture

Use this icon to make the selected object(s) into a picture.

Editing an Imported Picture

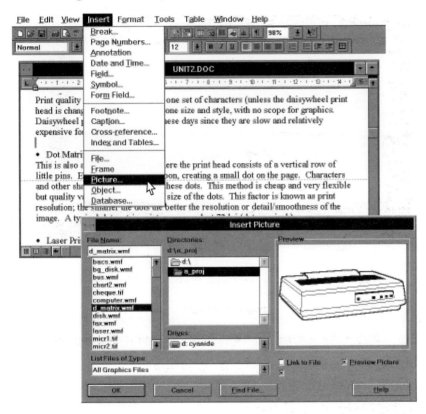

1. Import a clipart picture as normal, using the "Picture" option from the Insert menu.

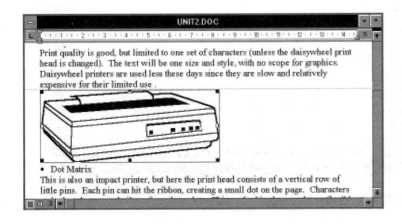

2.   Double-click on the Picture.

A new Draw window opens.

3.   Edit the shape. In this example we ungrouped, applied a
      grey fill, moved one polygon and reshaped another:

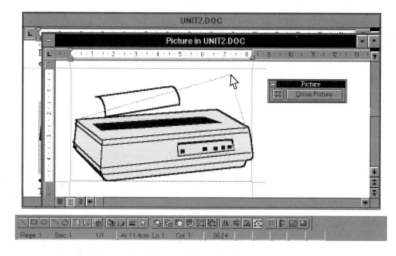

4.   Click on "Close" in the floating palette.

This returns you to the Word document.

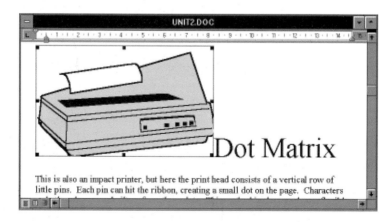

WordArt Special Effects

THIS CHAPTER COVERS

in easy steps

Insert Object

WordArt interfaces with Word using OLE (Object Linking and Embedding). Any application which supports OLE (e.g. Microsoft Excel or PowerPoint) will work in the same way.

1.   Choose "Object" from the Insert menu.

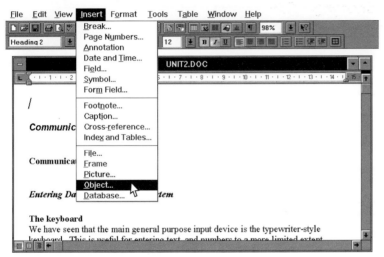

NOTE

WordArt is an added application that comes with Word. It is used to create intersting effects in your documents.

2.   Choose "Microsoft WordArt" from the Object Type list and click "OK".

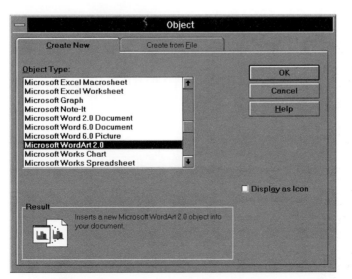

Microsoft WordArt will then take control...

Entering Text

Enter your text in the floating window:

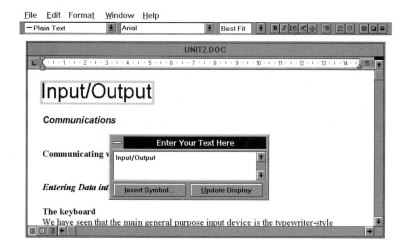

Choosing an Effect

Select a text effect from the drop-down list.

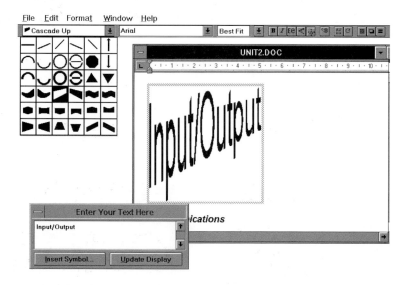

Example Effects

Triangle (Inverted)

Circle (Pour)

Wave2

Inflate (Top)

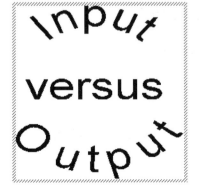

Button (Curve)

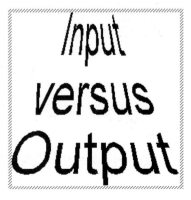

Fade Up

The Special Effects Box

1.   Choose "Rotation and Effects" from the Format menu:

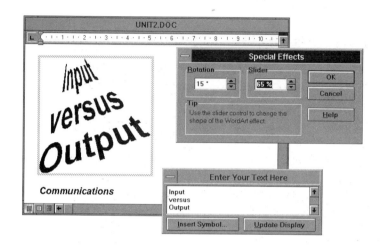

Spacing Between Characters

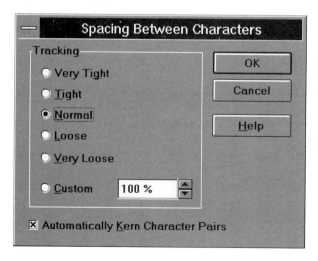

This can also be accessed from the Format menu.

Shading

"Shading", another option from the Format menu, is useful if you don't want the text solid black.

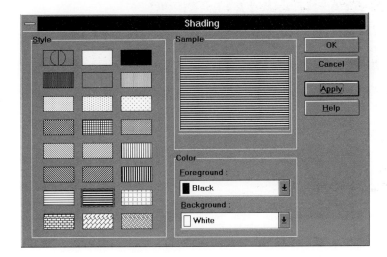

NOTE

Most of these options are also accessible from the WordArt toolbar at the top of the window area.

Shadow

You can access this option either from the toolbar or the Format menu.

When you've finished, click anywhere on the page (outside the WordArt text) to return to normal Word operation.

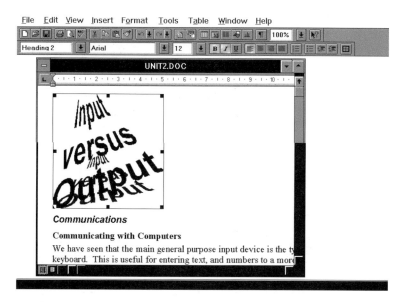

CHAPTER

23

Advanced
Features

Master Documents

Large documents slow down your machine, and are difficult to manage on your disk. Word's Master Document feature allows you to construct a document from many sources, whilst still retaining the benefits of a single file.

Master document view is an enhanced version of the Outliner (see Chapter 15).

Master Document View   *¡) select   VIEW , OUTLINE*

1.a) Choose "Master Document" from the View menu.

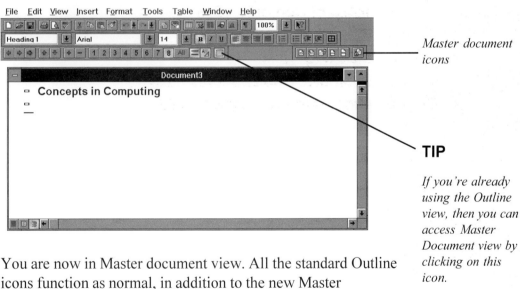

Master document icons

TIP

If you're already using the Outline view, then you can access Master Document view by clicking on this icon.

You are now in Master document view. All the standard Outline icons function as normal, in addition to the new Master Document icons in the toolbar.

Inserting a Subdocument

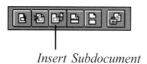

Insert Subdocument

1.　Click on the Insert Subdocument icon:

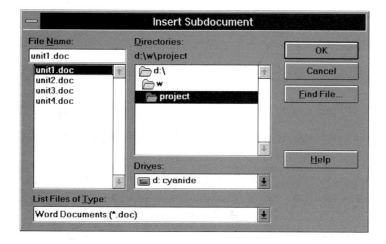

2.　Locate the required file and click "OK".　*OPEN*

Subdocument icon ———

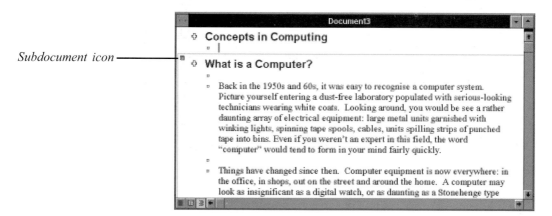

Although apparently part of the Master Document, this is still stored as a separate file on disk, and only accessed when needed.

Viewing the Structure

3.   Click on the level 2 icon to view the document using the first two levels of heading only:

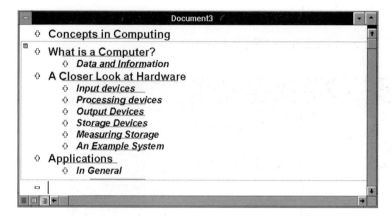

4.   Repeat this process to insert all the subdocuments needed.

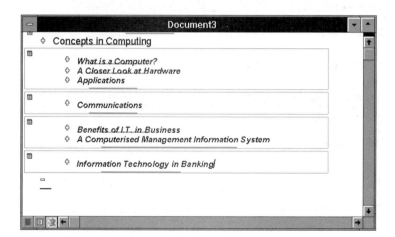

Creating a Subdocument

1.   Enter the text as normal.

2.   Select the text:

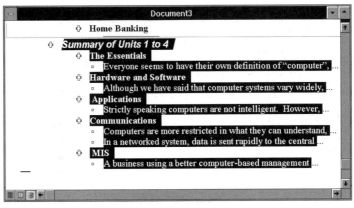

3.   Click on the Create Subdocument icon.

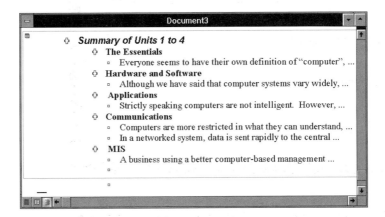

Creating Several Subdocuments at Once

4.   Select a series of major headings.

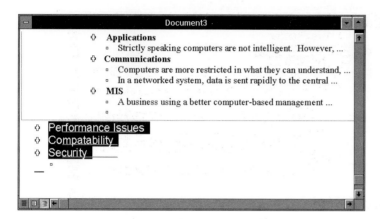

5.   Click on the Subdocument icon:

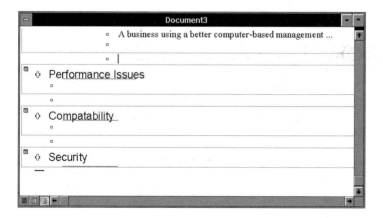

Each heading (plus its associated text) becomes a separate subdocument.

Deleting a Subdocument

1. Select the Subdocument by clicking on its main icon.

click here ———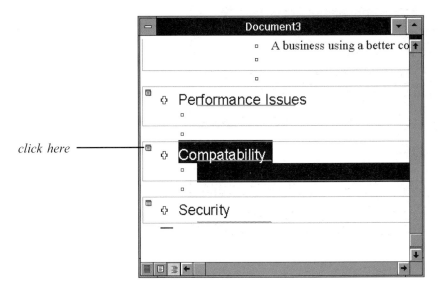

2. Press the Delete key.

The subdocument is deleted.

Merging Subdocuments

1. Select two adjacent subdocuments.

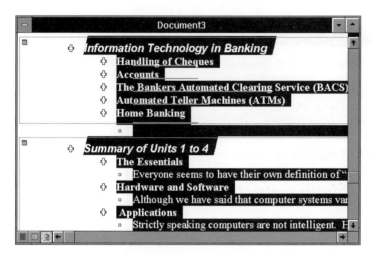

2. Click on the Merge Subdocuments icon.

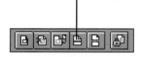

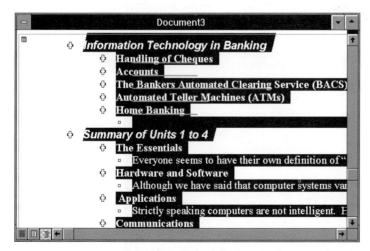

The two Subdocuments are joined as one.

Splitting Subdocuments

1. Click an Insertion Point inside a subdocument, at the point
    where you would like to divide it in two.

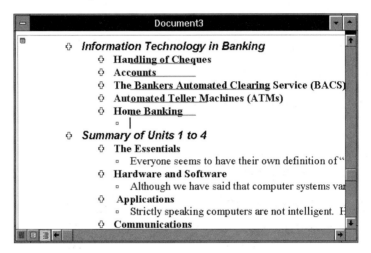

2. Click on the Split Subdocuments icon.

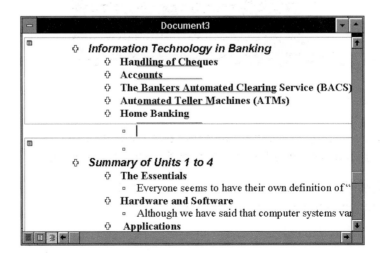

Locking a Subdocument

Because a subdocument is stored as a separate file, anyone could open it and make changes. This will obviously affect your Master Document in turn.

To prevent this happening, you can lock a subdocument:

1.　Select the subdocument.

2.　Click on the Lock Subdocument icon.

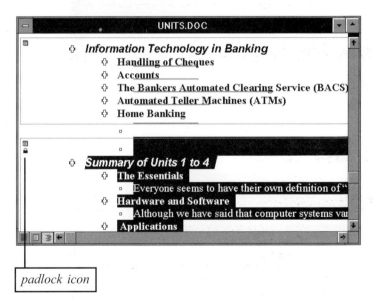

padlock icon

A padlock icon appears, to remind you that the document is locked. It can now only be edited from the Master document.

To unlock the subdocument simply click on the Lock Subdocument icon a second time.

Merging a Subdocument Back into the Main Document

1.   Select the Subdocument.

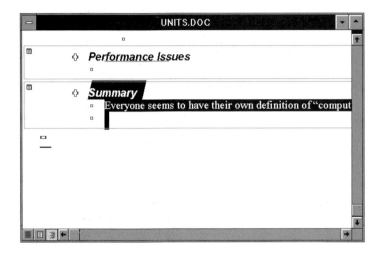

2.   Click on the Remove Subdocument icon.

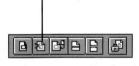

The text has now become part of the main document once again.

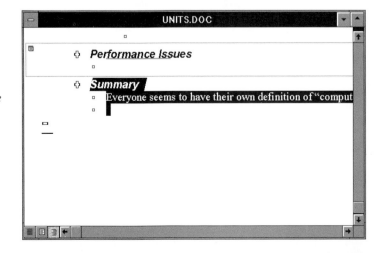

Behind the Scenes

Subdocuments are stored as separate files on disk:

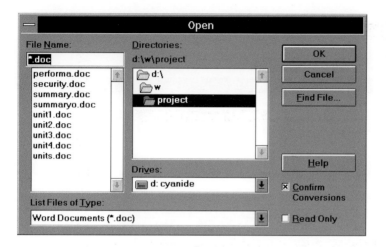

TIP

Try to organise your work so that all the subdocuments are stored in one directory specially set aside for this purpose.

In the above example all the ingredients are kept in a "PROJECT" directory, along with the Master document itself ("UNITS.DOC").

Bookmarks

Bookmarks are useful for quickly locating important parts of
your document. They are also used by some of the more
advanced automatic features, such as indexing.

Creating a Bookmark

1.   Select the text to be marked.

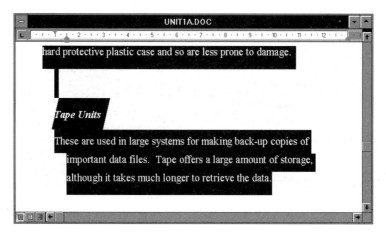

2.   Choose "Bookmark" from the Edit menu.

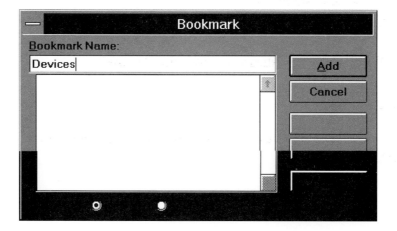

3.   Enter a name for your bookmark and then click "Add".

Using a Bookmark

Bookmarks can be made to show up from the Options menu (View tab). If this is active, then bookmarked text will be enclosed in square brackets [].

To locate a bookmark:

1.   Choose "Go to" from the Edit menu.

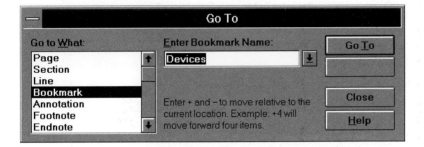

2.   Select "Bookmark" from the Go To What list.

3.   Type the Bookmark name or select it from the Enter Bookmark Name list.

4.   Click on "Go To".

5.   When you've finished searching, click "Close".

NOTE

You can also use the Go To dialog box to move to other locations, such as specific pages or sections.

Table of Contents

1.   Choose "Index and Tables" from the Insert menu.

2.   Select the "Table of Contents" tab.

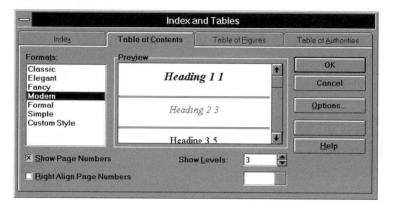

3.   Select the Format you require from the list.

4.   Click on "Options".

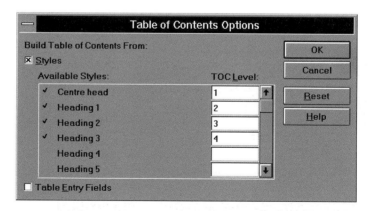

Table of Contents works by scanning through your document, looking for text using specific heading styles.

5.   Enter a level number for each style which you want to use.

The level number indicates the heading level of the entry in the Table of Contents.

6. Click "OK" to both dialog boxes.

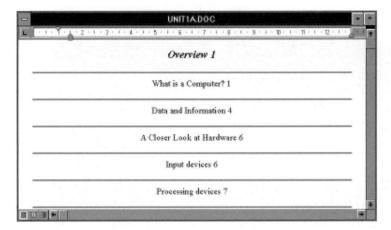

The Table of Contents appears at the current Insertion Point.

Changing the Table of Contents

1. Once again, choose "Index and Tables" from the Insert menu.

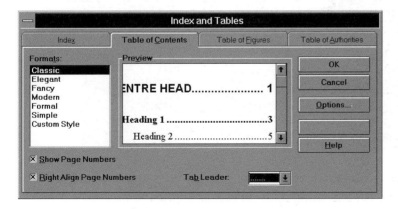

2. Experiment with different settings, referring to the Preview box for guidance.

3. Click "OK".

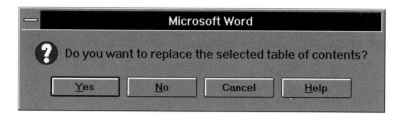

4.   Click "Yes" to the Warning dialog box.

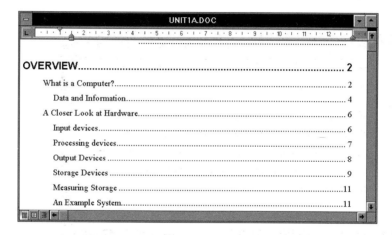

The Table of Contents is regenerated.

Manual Entries

Sometimes it is necessary to add Table of Contents entries which do not use a particular style in the main text.

To add a manual entry:

1. Click an Insertion Point at the desired point in the document.

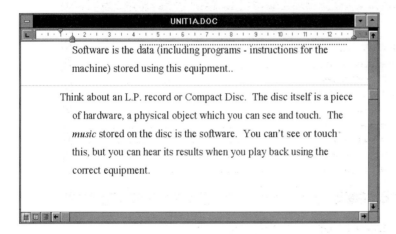

2. Choose "Field" from the Insert menu.

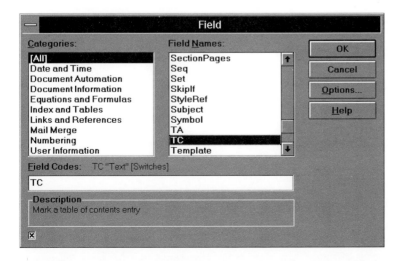

3.   Type or select "TC" as the field name.

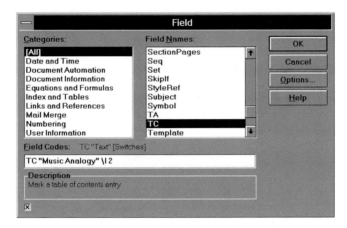

4.   After the "TC", leave a space and then type the name of the entry enclosed in quotation marks.

5.   Leave another space and then type a backslash followed by a letter "l" and a single digit representing the level number of the entry.

Example

TC "Music Analogy" \l2

...sets up a Table of Contents entry called "Music Analogy" which will appear as a level 2 entry.

6.   Click "OK".

The result in the document will look like this:

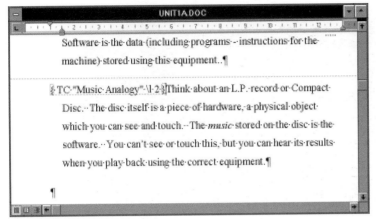

HINT

If you can't see the entry then choose "Options" from the Tools menu, click on the View tab and activate "Show Field Codes".

7. Now return to the Table of Contents dialog box (Insert menu).

8. Click on "Options".

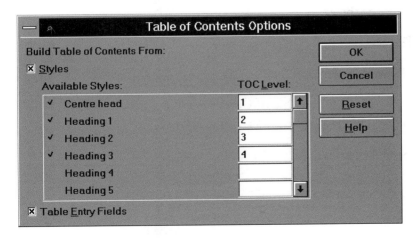

9. Activate the "Table Entry Fields" option.

10. Click "OK" to both dialog boxes.

The manual entry has now been included in the Table of Contents:

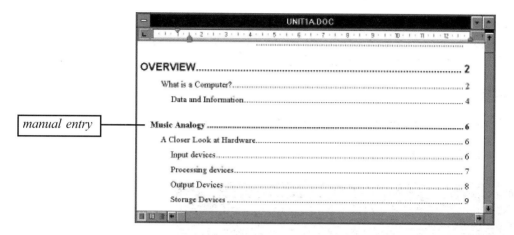

manual entry

TIP

You can customise further by editing the style definitions used by the Table of Contents. These are called "TOC 1", "TOC 2", "TOC 3" and so on.

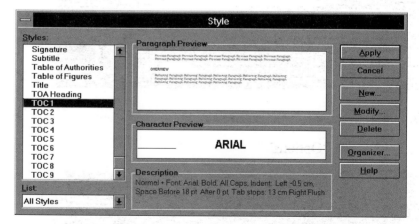

Other Types of Tables

You can also use the Index and Tables dialog to set up Tables of Authorities and Tables of Figures.

These both operate on the same principle as the Table of Contents, searching for styles or fields within your main text to compile the entries with their page references.

An example

1. Choose "Index and Tables" from the Insert menu.

2. Activate the "Table of Figures" tab.

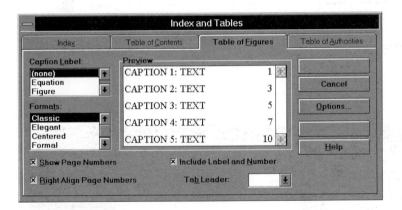

3. Choose the Caption Label and Formats option.

4. Click on "Options".

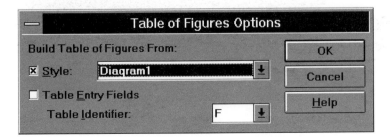

5. Select the Style or Entry Field to use, then click "OK" to both dialogs to generate the Table.

Indexing

Creating an Index can take a long time, but it is basically a
process of selecting text to be made into entries. In addition to
this you must choose the *type* of each index entry.

Creating an Entry

1.   Select the text to be made into an entry.

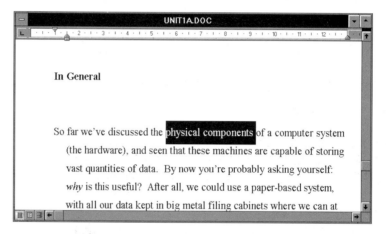

2.   Choose "Index and Tables" from the Insert menu.

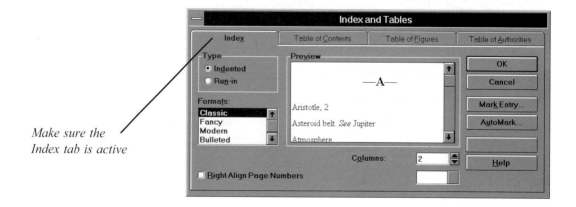

Make sure the
Index tab is active

3.   Click on "Mark Entry".

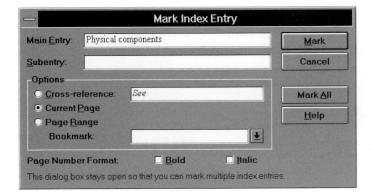

TIP

If you want to pick up all instances of the entry text, click on "Mark All" instead of "Mark".

4.   For a normal entry, simply click on "Mark".

Other Types of Entry

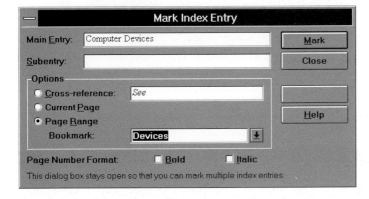

In this example, rather than seeing a single page reference in the index, we wanted a range of pages.

We did this by creating a Bookmark (see earlier in this chapter) to cover the range of text, and then selecting the Bookmark name within the Mark Index Entry dialog box.

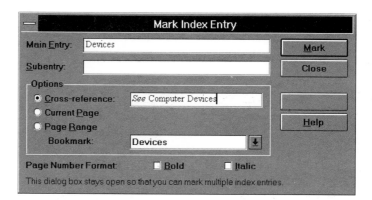

This is an example of a cross reference. To set this up click on "Cross-reference" and type the entry name in the box.

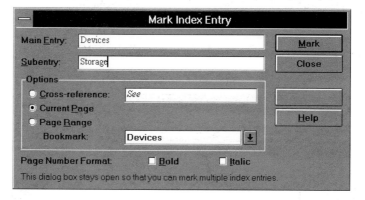

In this example we've created "Storage" as a sub-topic of "Devices".

Creating the Index

1.   Choose "Index and Tables" from the Insert menu.

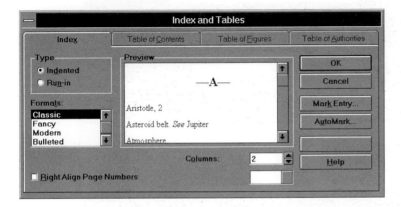

2.   Choose the Format for the Index, and click "OK".

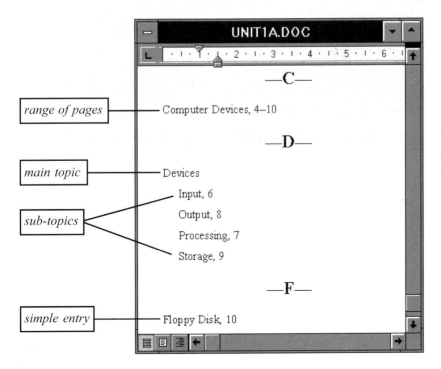

range of pages — Computer Devices, 4–10

main topic — Devices

sub-topics — Input, 6
Output, 8
Processing, 7
Storage, 9

simple entry — Floppy Disk, 10

The Index is generated at the current Insertion Point.

Using an AutoMark file

1. From the Index dialog box, click on "AutoMark".

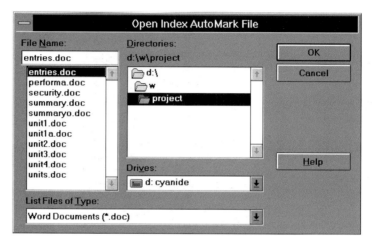

2. Select the AutoMark file and click "OK".

An AutoMark file is simply a text file containing words to be included in the Index.

You will need to prepare this yourself, but once this is done Word can search your main document for each entry included in the AutoMark file, and from this build up the complete Index.

Footnotes and Endnotes

Adding a Footnote or Endnote

1. Select the text which reference the footnote or endnote.

2. Choose "Footnote" from the Insert menu:

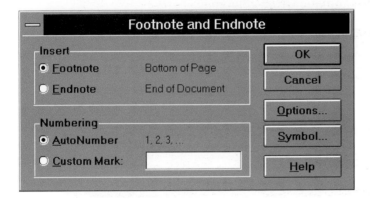

3. Select Footnote or Endnote and click "OK".

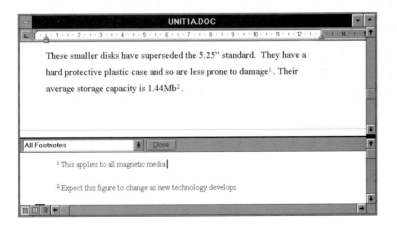

NOTE

Existing footnotes and endnotes are renumbered automatically each time you insert another.

The footnote or endnote is inserted into the footer area of the current page (footnote) or the end of the document (endnote).

Cross-reference Fields

Sometimes you need to refer to another part of your document. You could do this manually, but then you would need to keep track of page numbers. This is very tedious, particularly if the pages are renumbered frequently due to editing.

To add an automatic Cross-reference:

1. Enter the appropriate text, eg. "For more details about hardware devices, see page ".

2. Choose "Cross-reference" from the Insert menu.

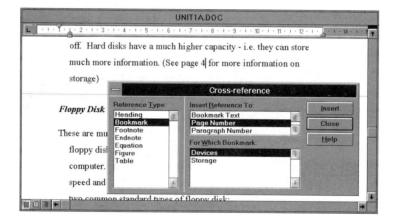

3. Choose what you would like to cross-reference. In this example it is a Bookmark named "Devices".

4. Click "Insert" then "Close".

The Cross-reference field is added to the document.

Customising Word

Macros

Macros allow you to make recordings of common activities, which can then be replayed whenever necessary.

1. Choose "Macro" from the Tools menu.

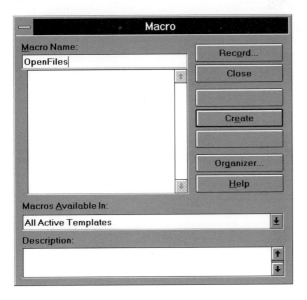

2. Enter the Macro name then click on "Record".

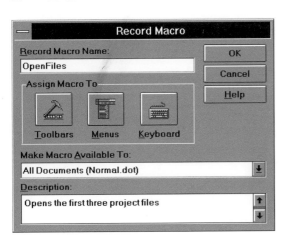

At this stage you could instruct Word to make your Macro part of a menu, toolbar or a keyboard command.

3. Click "OK".

All your actions are now being recorded...

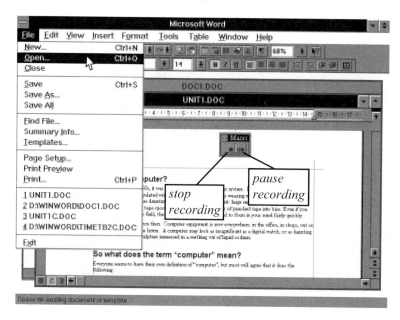

4.   Carry out all the actions to be recorded. When you've finished click on the "Stop Recording" icon in the floating Macro Record toolbar.

5.   Even if the Macro hasn't been assigned to a menu, toolbar or keyboard shortcut, you can still run it from the Macro dialog box ("Macro" from the Tools menu).

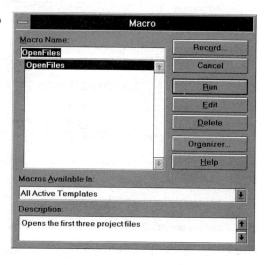

Customising Toolbars

1. Choose "Customise" from the Tools menu.

2. Make sure the "Toolbars" tab is active.

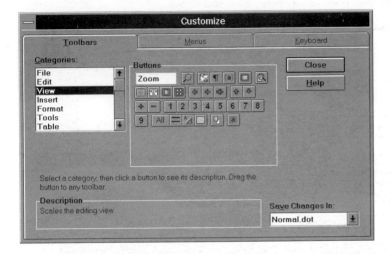

From this dialog you can choose which icons are to be included in each toolbar.

Customising Menus

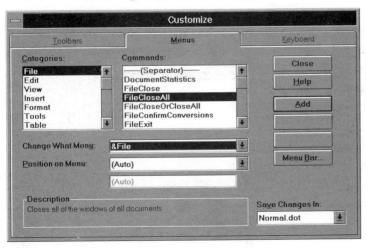

Click on the Menu tab to set up your own menu system.

Customising Keyboard Shortcuts

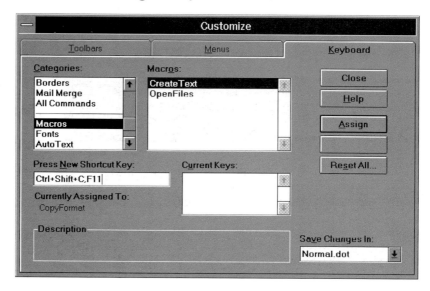

The Keyboard tab in the Customise dialog box allows you to assign a keyboard shortcut to virtually any action in Word.

NOTE

If you assign a keyboard shortcut already in use, your new option will override the old.

NORMAL.DOT

Saving changes to NORMAL.DOT (the default template) will change the global defaults for Word.

Symbols

1.   Choose "Symbol" from the Insert menu.

2.   If necessary, click on the "Symbols" tab.

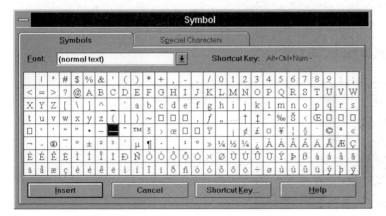

NOTE

These are the symbols available for the current font selected.

TIP

Click on a symbol to see it in a larger size.

From this dialog you can choose a symbol from the character map of any font installed on your system.

3.   Click on the "Special Characters" tab.

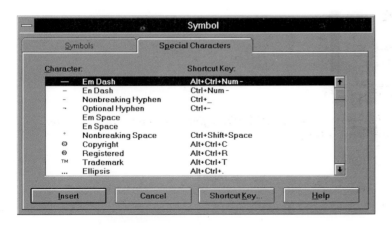

4.   Select the required character and click "Insert".

This will add the selected character or symbol at the Insertion point in your document.

Equations

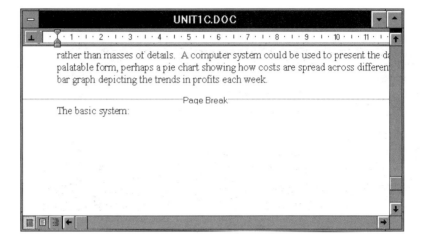

1.   Click the Insertion Point at the location for the equation.

Like WordArt, the Equation Editor uses OLE to communicate
with Word.

2.   Choose "Object" from the Insert menu.

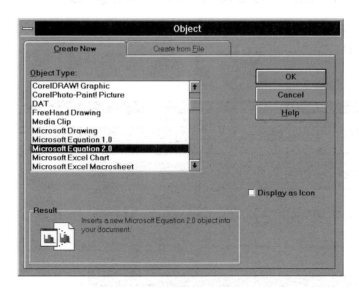

3.   Choose "Microsoft Equation" and click "OK".

The Equation Editor opens:

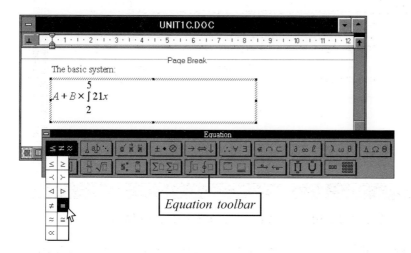

Equation toolbar

4. Enter your equation, using the Equation toolbar to insert special symbols and formatting options, as required.

5. Click anywhere on the page but outside the equation to return to normal Word operation.

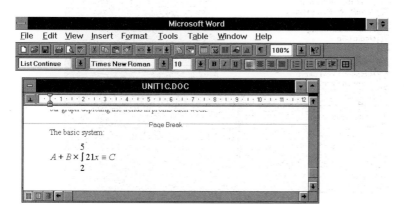

To return to the Equation editor at any time, simply double click on the Equation itself.

Performance Issues

If you find that Word runs slowly on your machine, here are a few tips to speed things up:

1.   Select Normal page view.

2.   Go to the Tools menu and choose "Options".

3.   From the View tab:

     •   Select "Draft font". Normal page view will now
         display all text in one font, regardless of formatting.
         You'll need to use Page Layout view to preview text
         effects.

     •   Select "Picture Placeholders". All pictures will be
         displayed as outlined boxes. Note this also affects
         Page Layout view.

4.   From the General tab:

     •   Deactivate "Background Pagination". Word will no
         longer continually calculate page breaks as you work.
         To check on pagination, switch to Page Layout or
         Print Preview.

5.   From the Save tab:

     •   Deselect "Automatic Save". This will stop
         interruptions to your work during which the file is
         saved periodically. Note that it is now up to you to
         ensure that important work is saved frequently.

Reference

Keyboard Shortcuts

Moving

Cursor keys	Up/down/left/right one space
Ctrl + left/right	Previous/next word
Ctrl + up/down	Previous/next paragraph
Home/End	Beginning/end of line
Ctrl + Home/End	Beginning/end of document
PgUp/PgDn	Move up/down one screen
Ctrl + PgUp/PgDn ...	Move to top/bottom of window
Alt+Shift+Up/Down .	Select paragraph and move up/down

Editing

Ctrl+NumPad5	Select entire document
Alt+Shift+NumPad5 (Numlock off)	Apply normal style
Return	New paragraph
Shift+Return	New line within paragraph
Ctrl+Return..............	New page
Ctrl+Shift+Return	New column
Ctrl+Shift+*	Display invisible characters
Ctrl+Backspace	Delete word to left
Ctrl+Delete	Delete word to right
Ctrl+Shift+C	Copy format
Ctrl+Shift+V	Paste format

Quick Formatting

Ctrl+B	Bold
Ctrl+I	Italic
Ctrl+Shift+A	All caps

Ctrl+Shift+K	Small caps
Ctrl+U	Normal underline
Ctrl+Shift+D	Double underline
Ctrl+Shift+W	Word underline
Ctrl+Shift+P	Enter point size
Ctrl+Shift+F	Enter font
Ctrl+=	Subscript
Ctrl and + ...	Superscript
Ctrl+Shift+>	Increase size
Ctrl+Shift+<	Decrease size
Ctrl+)	Increase by 1 point
Ctrl+(.......................	Decrease by 1 point
Ctrl+Shift+(..............	Kern together
Ctrl+Shift+)	Kern apart
Ctrl+Space	Reset format to current style
Ctrl+Shift+S	Select style
Ctrl+L	Left align
Ctrl+E	Centre align
Ctrl+R	Right align
Ctrl+J	Justify
Ctrl+M	Indent
Ctrl+Shift+M	Decrease indent
Ctrl+T	Hanging indent
Ctrl+Shift+T	Decrease hanging indent
Ctrl+1	Single line spacing
Ctrl+2	Double line spacing
Ctrl+5	1.5 line spacing
Ctrl+Shift+Q	Apply Symbol font

Menu Options

Ctrl+N	New
Ctrl+O	Open
Ctrl+W	Close
Ctrl+S	Save
Ctrl+P	Print
Ctrl+Z	Undo
Ctrl+Y	Redo
Ctrl+X	Cut

◁

Ctrl+C	Copy
Ctrl+V	Paste
Ctrl+A	Select All
Ctrl+F	Find
Ctrl+H	Replace
Ctrl+G	Go To
Alt+Ctrl+N	Normal view
Alt+Ctrl+O	Outline
Alt+Ctrl+P	Page Layout
Alt+Shift+R	Headers/footers
Ctrl+D	Font dialog
Ctrl+K	AutoFormat

Function Keys

F1	Help
Shift+F1	Context sensitive help
F2	Move selected text
Shift+F2	Copy selected text
Ctrl+F2	Print preview
F3	Glossary entry
Shift+F3	Change case
Ctrl+F3	Cut to spike
Ctrl+Shift+F3	Insert spike
F4	Repeat previous command
Shift+F4	Find/Go To again
Ctrl+F4	Close document window
Alt+F4	Exit
F5	Go To
Shift+F5	Go back
Ctrl+F5	Restore document window
Ctrl+Shift+F5	Bookmark
Alt+F5	Restore Word window
F6	Next pane
Shift+F6	Previous pane
Ctrl+F6	Next document window

Ctrl+Shift+F6	Previous document window
F7	Spelling
Shift+F7	Thesaurus
Ctrl+F7	Move document window
Ctrl+Shift+F7	Update links
F8	Extend selection
Shift+F8	Reduce selection
Ctrl+F8	Resize document window
Ctrl+Shift+F8	Select column
F9	Update field
Shift+F9	Display selected field on/off
Ctrl+F9	Insert field manually
Ctrl+Shift+F9	Unlink field
Alt+F9	Display all fields on/off
Alt+Shift+F9	Activate field
F10	Activate menu
F11	Next field
Shift+F11	Previous field
Ctrl+F11	Lock field
Ctrl+Shift+F11	Unlock field
F12	Save as
Shift+F12	Save
Ctrl+F12	Open
Ctrl+Shift+F12	Print

Special Characters

Ctrl+Shift+Space	Nonbreaking space
Ctrl+Hyphen	Optional hyphen
Ctrl+Shift+Hyphen	Nonbreaking hyphen
Ctrl+Tab	Insert Tab (into table)
Alt+0xxxx (on numeric keypad)	Insert ANSI character code xxxx

Tips for Good Document Design

- Try not to use too many fonts or text effects. Often good results can be gained from restricting yourself to two basic fonts, one for headings and one for body text.

- Allow yourself the use of white space. It is usually not necessary to completely fill the page, and space can be used as a very effective way of adding emphasis.

- Make sure that your text is always readable. More than 40 characters (or 10 words) to a line puts a strain on the human eye. Also too little space between lines can create a solid mass of text which is very tiring to read.

- Use Styles as much as possible. This way you have the flexibility to make design alterations to, for example, all your headings in one simple manoeuvre at any time.

- Make sure your document has a clear structure. In particular check that main headings are obviously more prominent than sub-headings.

- Check the available Templates to see if there is a ready-made document which suits your purposes. If not, you may still be able to adapt an existing Template in order to create your own.

- Feel free to experiment with dummy text and graphics in the early stages of your design. Try to form a clear idea of which settings to use for document margins, text columns and page structure right from the beginning of your work.

- Keep your design as simple and consistent as possible.

Index

Other Books from Computer Step

The PC Novice's Handbook 2nd edition by Harshad Kotecha
ISBN 1-874029-04-0
128 pages £9.95

The PC Novice's Handbook for Upgrading & Maintenance by Roy Bunce and Frances Maddison
ISBN 1-874029-14-8
160 pages £9.95

The Complete Guide to Sage Sterling & Accounting by Stephen Jay (foreword GT)
ISBN 1-874029-10-5
468 pages £19.95

The Complete Guide to Sage Sterling+2 for Windows by Adele Ward ISBN 1-874029-17-2
248 pages £14.95

Computers in Schools by Steve Greenwood ISBN 1-874029-05-9
144 pages £5.95

Computing for the Terrified! by Steve Greenwood ISBN 1-874029-09-1
151 pages £6.95

WordPerfect: The Joy of Six by Darren Ingram ISBN 1-874029-08-3
155 pages £11.95

I Wanna know all about PCs by John H.Sumner ISBN 1-874029-20-2
282 pages £14.95

Discover PageMaker Scripting by Andrew Bennett ISBN 1-874029-22-9
160 pages £16.95

in easy Steps *books on next page (PTO)*

Other in easy steps Books

by Harshad Kotecha 1-874029-18-0 128pp £9.95

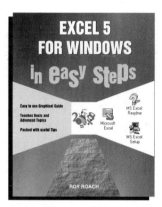

by Roy Roach 1-874029-15-6 316pp £14.95

by Harshad Kotecha 1-874029-12-1 180pp £14.95

by Kate Stewart 1-874029-11-3 331pp £14.95

by Scott Basham 1-874029-19-9 220pp £14.95

For further information please contact:

5c Southfield Road Southam
Warwickshire CV33 OJH
England
Tel 01926 817999 Fax 01926 817005